THE SIXTY MINUTE MOTHER

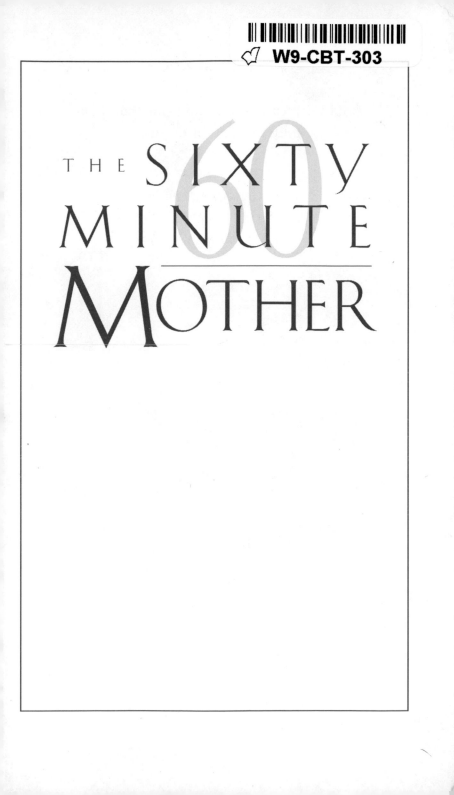

The "Sixty-Minute" Series

Books you can read in an hour that make
a lifetime of difference.

The Sixty-Minute Father
The Sixty-Minute Marriage
The Sixty-Minute Mother

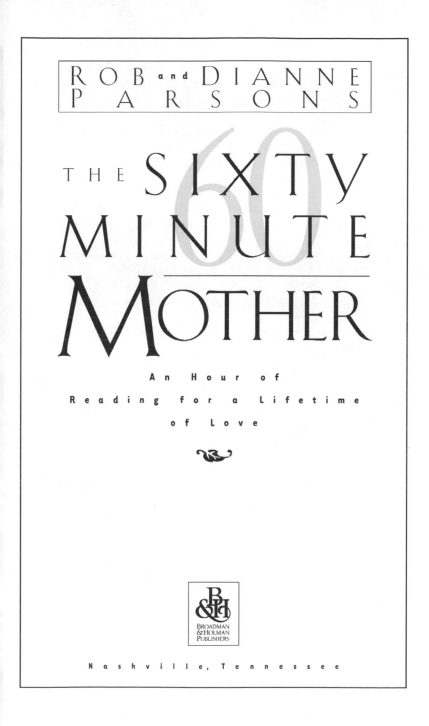

ROB and DIANNE PARSONS

THE SIXTY 60 MINUTE MOTHER

An Hour of
Reading for a Lifetime
of Love

BROADMAN
&HOLMAN
PUBLISHERS

Nashville, Tennessee

© 2002 by Rob and Dianne Parsons
All rights reserved
Printed in the United States of America

0-8054-2556-X
Published by Broadman & Holman Publishers,
Nashville, Tennessee
First published in Great Britain, 2000,
by Hodder & Stoughton, London

Dewey Decimal Classification: 306.874
Subject Heading: PARENTING—MOTHERS
Library of Congress Card Catalog Number: 2001052549

Published in association with Alive Communications, Inc.,
7680 Goddard St.. Ste. 200, Colorado Springs, Colorado, 80920

Library of Congress Cataloging-in-Publication Data
Parsons, Rob, 1948–
    The sixty-minute mother : an hour of reading for a lifetime of
love / Rob and Dianne Parsons.
        p. cm.
    Originally published: Great Britain : Hodder & Stoughton,
2000.
    ISBN 0-8054-2556-X (pb.)
    1. Mother and child. 2. Mothers—Psychology. 3. Mother—
Attitudes. 4. Parenting. I. Parsons, Dianne, 1949– II. Title.
    HQ759 .P288 2002
    306.874'3—dc21

                                                          2001052549
                                                          CIP

1 2 3 4 5 6 7 8 9 10   06 05 04 03 02

Dedication

To Lyndon and Celia Bowring

For the years of wisdom, encouragement,
and friendship—thank you.

Who ran to help me when I fell,
And would some pretty story tell,
Or kiss the place to make it well?
My mother.

Anne Taylor, *Original Poems*

A mother is neither cocky nor proud because she knows
that the school headmaster may call at any minute to
report that her child has just driven a motorcycle
through the school gymnasium.

Mary Kay Blakely

Acknowledgments

Wendy Bray and Jill Worth have been with us on this project since the beginning. They have advised us, guided us, helped us gather material from other mothers and written some of the *Take a Break* sections. Jill is a single-parent mom of Sophie, age fifteen, and Thomas, age eight. Wendy is married to Richard and has two children: Lois, age thirteen, and Benjamin, age ten. As we write, she is in the middle of intensive chemotherapy and shares something of her story in the chapter titled "When a Mother Is Sick."

Sheron Rice, our assistant, has shown commitment to this project and patience beyond the call of duty. That was no surprise to us; Sheron has recently lost her own mother and could not have had a better mother or loved her more. Her contribution to this book was literally a labor of love dedicated on behalf of her and her sister Joy to the memory of their mom.

Thank you also to Lisa Curtis, Tom Beardshaw, Celia Bowring, Lyndon Bowring, Caroline Adams, Kate Hancock, Gill Williams, and Steve Williams. Jonathan Booth has played his normal role of sergeant-major and therapist.

Janis Whipple and the team at Broadman & Holman have been brilliant as ever—supportive, encouraging, and patient!

And, above all, gratitude to the mothers who contributed—to protect privacy we have sometimes changed your names but not your stories.

Contents

CHAPTER ONE

Motherhood— the Truth Is Out

Shortly after Rob wrote *The Sixty-Minute Father,* two things began to happen. First, mothers began to write to him saying how much they enjoyed it and that really it was a book for them as well. Second, all the research we were able to do showed us it was *mothers* who were mainly buying it and leaving it around for the men in their lives to read!

Over the past twelve years, over two hundred thousand people have attended the family seminars at which we speak. The vast proportion of these are mothers. During the coffee breaks it is invariably mothers who wait to speak with us; this is true whether we are in Paris, Moscow, Vancouver, or Manchester. Every year tens of thousands of people contact us in relation to our work with families; the majority of them are mothers. Much of our work has been with single parents—for the past five years we have organized vacations specifically for single parents and their families—and again most are mothers.

We have listened to moms who feel they have blown it irretrievably; to "stay at home" moms who wonder whether people think they have taken a soft option, and to working moms who are struggling with a demanding toddler and an even more demanding boss—both of them have learned how to stamp their feet when they don't get what they want. We have listened to moms who think they are the only ones whose baby won't sleep at night and to mothers of teenagers who feel they are the only parents in the world whose child sits next to them for the whole school journey without saying a word.

We have been in a very privileged position. Thousands of mothers have written to us, often spoken with us, and told us of lessons they have learned. Many have said, "I wish someone had told me about some of this when my kids were small, but I learned it the hard way." In *The Sixty-Minute Mother* we wanted to pass on some of what those moms have told us—lessons in the art of motherhood.

Every so often you'll see a *Take a Break* section. This is a chance to put the coffee on and just relax as all kinds of moms share what they have learned over the years and, just as important . . . *how they feel*. And once in a while there is a *Sixty-Second Wisdom* page from mothers who have seen it all, done it all.

Almost every mother we have ever met acknowledges motherhood as a joyful, painful, exciting, mind-numbing business, and above all, as a long-haul affair. No matter how old our children are, it seems the task of parenthood never ends. Fifteen years ago a mother who was ninety-five years old came into Rob's office. She said to him, "I can rest in peace now, my boy." He said, "Oh, why is that?" She replied, "Because I've just managed to get my youngest son into an old people's home." It turned out that he was seventy-two and a bit shaky. But she was in full control of all her faculties and having got him started in school, university, and marriage, was now tying up the last few ends—*as a mother.*

"Sometimes I don't like my kids!"

Sometime over the next few days, go to your child's bedroom and take the dog-eared copy of *Children's Best-Loved Stories* off the bookshelf. Now turn to "The Emperor's New Clothes," put the coffee on and read. When you get to the part where the small boy yells, "The king is naked!" imbibe the honesty, let it seep into your very soul, set down your coffee, and run into the streets yelling, "Being a mother is hard!" "Sometimes I don't like my kids!" "Sometimes I wish I hadn't had my kids." And as you shout, turn around, for you will see behind you thousands of mothers joining in the procession and all of them with a look of utter joy on their faces, not for the fact that they have found solutions, but for the sheer wonder that at long last the truth is out.

It was Bill Cosby who said, "I guess the real reason that my wife and I had children is the same reason that Napoleon had for invading Russia: it seemed like a good idea at the time. Since then, however, I've had some doubts, primarily about my intelligence."

We often meet mothers who feel that way. They are, simply, discouraged. And they are tired: tired of worrying, tired of getting the blame for all the ills in their kids' lives—from warts to failed examinations—and tired of feeling guilty. Occasionally a mom will confide the heartrending realization that she wishes she had never had children to begin with. She carries this thought like a scar, for it is mingled with unbelievable love for her child.

One mother put it like this:

> *My life took on the feeling of a monotonous routine, made even more difficult with the baby's bouts of colic. They seemed to occur every night between eleven and three in the morning. One long night as I paced the floor trying to calm my screaming baby, uncontrollable tears started to flow down my face. I was slowly hit with the realization that the fun and games were ended and we weren't playing house any more. The reality hit me with a stunning blow.*

It can be so very hard coming to terms with all of this. Society keeps telling us that parenthood is the ultimate privilege, but why then do parents often feel what appears to be sheer misery? The answer is not that we are failures, simply that we are feeling the effect of complete responsibility for the life of another person, over whom we have no final control, and who seems only intermittently to either want our involvement or to be in the least grateful for it.

We have several hopes for this book. We want us to laugh together, and we want all kinds of mothers to yell out, "Thank goodness this is not just me." We want single-parent moms to feel encouraged and not marginalized. We want moms who feel like failures to be inspired not to give up. And, above all, we want mothers to feel honored and respected. It was Gerald Ford, former president of the United States, who said, "You can hold high office, but when your time is over, the world will forget you." That is not true of motherhood: your kids will remember you forever.

A Word from Rob . . .

I have spoken with thousands of mothers, but I have only had the opportunity to observe two at close quarters.

The first is now ninety years old. My abiding memory is of her clearing tables in the restaurant of a large store so she could get enough money together by Christmas to buy me the chemistry set that sat proudly on the shelf in the toy department. She had no formal education to speak of, but she possessed a wisdom that seemed at times almost from another world. If she had any fault, it was probably that she loved her children too much—to the exclusion of all else. I have always feared the day she would die, but, in truth, I have gotten used to losing my mother. About three years ago her mind became very confused. I went to visit one day, and she said, "How are you, son?"

"Oh," I replied, "not bad—I'm a bit worried about the kids." I waited for her normal wisdom, but instead she looked up and said, "I'm having my hair done today." And suddenly she was gone—oh, still present, but lost to me. I have grieved for her over three years. She is a wonderful mother.

The second, of course, is my wife, Dianne. We have been married for almost thirty years. She is an unusual mother; she had to be. Dianne has not only cared for our children, Katie and Lloyd, but for Ron who is four years older than us. He spent most of his young life in the care of the local authority, and we knew him when we were in our teens. He was pretty well homeless when he knocked on our door one night near Christmas. Dianne asked him to stay the night with us. That was twenty-five years ago, and he has never left. He has been with us longer than the kids. She jokes that she practiced on Ron and it gave her a head start. Dianne is one of the most honest people I know, and I thought a wonderful way to start our time together would be to ask an honest mother to share some memories.

CHAPTER TWO

When a Mother Remembers

Dianne Parsons

I often have to drive past the elementary school that my children attended. My daughter Katie is now twenty-two, my son Lloyd, nineteen, and yet I only have to glance at the gates at the end of the play-ground for a million memories to come flooding back. Suddenly it is a crisp September morning and it is my daughter's first day at school. We walk from our home together, her hand tightly gripping mine. The excitement and bravado of this step into the world of the "big kids" seem to desert her the moment we close the front door, and now she looks white and worried and I catch her nibbling her bot-tom lip—a sure sign that tears are close at hand.

I edge her down the road toward the school and talk of anything except this special day. She mumbles replies, but I catch her watching the other children to whom this is all old hat; the kids who jostle us are seven-year-old veterans. She begins to slow her step, and I begin to fear the worst when suddenly an angel appears, or so it seems to me.

Actually it is her best friend for whom this is also the first day. Suddenly Katie leaves my side and runs toward Rhian. I am left standing, watching as these two little girls walk solemnly up the school drive together, holding hands and each clutching a "My Little Pony" lunch box. I feel my eyes fill up and then Katie turns and shouts, "See you later, Mom!" Against all the predictions my shy, careful child has done it. She has begun.

And then my mind fast-forwards three years. It is Lloyd's first day. The parenting gurus tell us that if your first child is shy, careful, and compliant your second will be different. Lloyd was desperate not to disappoint those experts. In fact, he dedicated most of his young life to proving them correct in every detail. I knew his first day of school would be quite different; I just didn't have any idea how different.

In an event never to be repeated, he was up and dressed before me and hammering on my bedroom door yelling, "Come on, I want to get there early!" As I had with Katie, I took his hand as we walked down the road together. But whereas Katie had found this comforting, Lloyd looked as though somebody had tethered him to a walking embarrassment. He dragged me toward the place of learning, firing off threatening glances at children twice his size, and with a burst of impatience, finally broke loose and ran ahead. I turned a corner and saw he was almost at the gate. And then it happened. He took one look into the playground, grimaced at a teacher, and then slowly walked back to me and said, "I'm not going."

I immediately clicked into my, "No-pain-no-gain," "You'll-be-sorry-when-you're-thirty," and "Superman-went-to-school" routine. He looked up with that little jaw set in the now-familiar look of defiance and repeated, "I'm not going." And so the battle began. There were moments over the next ten minutes when it seemed possible that with the aid of other mothers I would loosen his grip on the lamppost. But he held firm. The prospect of Lloyd beginning his formal education linked to twenty feet of vertical concrete with a light on top was rushing through my brain when the assistant principal appeared.

I have never managed to work out whether her concern was for me, Lloyd, or the property of the county council, but she ordered me to leave. I will never forget Lloyd's face. He was torn between running after me—which meant giving up his hold on the lamppost—or remaining within the influence of a woman who looked decidedly less sympathetic to the plight of small boys than his mother. He hesitated and I went—not willingly, but propelled along by Sheila Harrison, who had done all this four times already. As she whisked me away she said, "He'll be better off without you." I have since wondered whether she meant just at that moment or in life generally.

But on that morning, at least, she was right and I had finally ushered my two children into the "real" world. How was I to know that motherhood involves a million schoolyard experiences at every age and that the process was only just starting? Why didn't somebody tell me? I'll tell you the reason— because if they had, you'd have never gotten *me* off that lamppost!

The Way We Were

As I look back on my kids' lives, so many recollections come flooding back.

Every time early September comes, with the first hint of autumn crispness, I am immediately transported to the maternity ward and Katie's birth. I remember lying there, having gone in early with high blood pressure, and wondering what motherhood was going to be like.

And I remember another autumn morning just after Lloyd was born. Katie was a toddler and my new son was asleep in the room next to me. It was about seven in the morning and the sun was streaming through the curtains. It was in so many ways a perfect day. I had two children, a lovely home, and a good husband. But none of that seemed to be very real at that moment and I turned, woke Rob, and said, "I don't think I can cope anymore. Will you take Katie to nursery today?"

Those words ushered in some dark years for Rob and me. I've no doubt that what they call post-partum depression was part of it, but the doctors also found a problem with my immune system. Some days I would just lie in bed. Most friends were kind; others had advice on how to "snap out of it" and reminded me that there were those who were a lot worse off than me. The strange thing is that the main emotion I felt was not sadness or worry but guilt. Why couldn't I cope? What would all this do to my children? Why wasn't I a better mother?

I would love to put my arms around young mothers going through similar experiences and tell them that they can come through these dark times. I would love to explain to spouses what is going on and urge them to both care and be patient. I now have the opportunity to speak to thousands of women through our seminars and perhaps it's as well that autumn morning is still fresh in my mind. It has left me vulnerable and therefore, I think, understanding.

I feel that illness robbed me of quite a lot of Lloyd's young life, but I still have some wonderful memories: one is of him giggling. He had such an infectious giggle. Sometimes I would be so angry with him, but against all my will he'd make me laugh.

I remember the joy of him when he was so very tactile, and even up until he was twelve he would lie with me on the sofa and link his arm through mine. And I remember the feeling almost of grief in his teenage years when that suddenly stopped and it appeared he didn't want to be seen out with me unless I had a brown paper bag over my head. And I remember when in his later teens I saw the first signs of a thaw after such a long winter and how it warmed my heart.

I remember Lloyd telling me he would never marry anybody else except me, and both my kids telling me when they were young that they would never leave home. And I remember, when they were teenagers, worrying in case they meant it.

I remember being a little overweight (what do I mean "remember," I *am* a little overweight!) and Katie asking me to go shopping with her—that's "size four" Katie. We both took clothes into the changing rooms. I nearly brought the wall of the dressing room down after losing my balance trying to get into a skirt I should have known was a size too small. And then when I was at my lowest, red-faced and depressed, the curtain went back and Katie stood there looking absolutely stunning in a little black number and said, "Does my bottom look big in this?" I wanted to attack her.

I remember being jealous if they went through times when they communicated with Rob more than me. I remember being desperately hurt if they didn't want to eat the meals I'd prepared. And I remember that no matter what they had done to me during the day, and no matter how old they were, it was impossible not to feel tremendous love for them when they were asleep.

And I remember times of helpless laughter. The other day I got my little family around me and said, "I have some important information to impart; listen well." Rob said, "Does this include me?" I said, "Especially you." Without pausing for breath I went on, "It appears that there are some things in this house that only I can do. In case I get hit by a bus, I want to pass on the wisdom of the years to you." They stood there open-mouthed.

"Today's lesson is how to replace a used toilet roll. The first part is to notice the empty roll on the holder. Unless you remove it, it will not self-destruct. Push the spindle gently and remove the empty roll. Put it in the trash can, *not* on the windowsill—we've stopped collecting them for crafts at school. Now, here's the really hard part: push the spindle again and put a new roll on. There! Now you can try it on your own next time."

I am a mother. I am not a perfect mother—I learned a long time ago that "perfect" is too great a burden to carry. Nor am I "just" a mother. I am a woman with gifts, hopes, and desires that are unconnected to my two kids. But, without doubt, it is in the realm of motherhood that you will find my greatest laughter and my deepest sorrow; it is there you will discover my greatest pride and haunting fears.

Sixty-Second Wisdom

*(from mothers who've seen it all, done it all,
worn the T-shirt . . . and survived!)*

60 Guilt is an occupational hazard; learn to live with it—it comes with the placenta.

60 Ignore the dust occasionally; or, better still, teach them how to spell in it!

60 Don't be too upset when your kids don't want the meal you made. I know it doesn't help when your son comes home and says, "Tom's mom made us eggs on toast." You say, "But you don't like eggs!" and he replies, "I do now." It *is* hurtful, but it's not personal.

60 Two-year-olds are not fooled by designs of a clown with a mashed potato face, a sausage nose, pea eyes, a carrot smile, and broccoli hair. They *know* what broccoli is.

You're Not the Only Mother Who . . .

- Says as she cleans out the rabbit, hamster, and bird cages, "Why do I fall for it time and time again?"

- Thinks she's on a game show, where the prize goes to the mother who can find the most dirty dishes in the shortest time, including those in her teenager's closet.

- Honestly believes that if she were introduced to the president, he would say, "Nice to see you, Mrs. Harries. You haven't seen my Game Boy anywhere, have you?"

- Turns her daughter's dirty white socks inside out so they look clean for Brownies.

- Stays up all night making a dozen brownies for the school bake sale and then, on seeing that Danielle Thomas's mother has made a novelty cake in the shape of a treehouse—complete with squirrel—goes straight home and eats all the brownies.

The First Child

I felt as though I had been in labor for most of my life, but really it was only seven hours before I heard a cry from my newborn baby daughter. Elated and relieved at the safe arrival of our much-wanted first child, my husband, Michael, and I wept as together we held the baby.

But two hours later, in the hospital room, my elation gave way to panic. Gazing at my daughter, I was overwhelmed by the responsibility of having my own child. I thought, *This is it now—there's no going back. She's mine for the rest of my life.*

My baby opened her eyes, and we stared at each other. I was the one to blink first. *What have I done?* I thought. *And where is the joy and happiness everyone told me I'd be feeling? What's wrong with me—aren't I a normal mother?*

Alison, mother of Rebecca

Nursery School

My child's nursery school has a box that contains spare underwear for children who haven't quite mastered the art of getting to the bathroom on time. The other day, Emma, my three-year-old, wore a pair home. I washed them and gave them to my husband to return to the nursery when he dropped her off the next day. He was sitting on the bus with Emma when a helper from the nursery got on, smiled at them and sat down at the back. A few minutes passed, and then Emma stood up, turned around, and, to the amusement of the crowded bus, said, "It's all right, Miss Deverold. My father's got your underwear in his pocket."

CHAPTER THREE

When a Mother Accepts

"What is the greatest gift a mother can give a child?" That was the question asked of four hundred women at a recent seminar. The most common reply, by far, was "love."

We're not at all sure it is the right answer. If it is, then we should be pleased, for although most of us have critics, enemies, and those who find us just plain irritating, our mothers love us. One of the most embarrassing moments of Rob's life occurred at 10:30 on a winter's morning when he was thirty-nine years old. At that time he was a senior partner in a legal practice and had a rather pompous and crusty bank manager as a passenger in his car. As they made their way along a busy street Rob saw his mother shopping. She would have been almost eighty then and was struggling with a large bag in the rain. "That's my mother over there," Rob said to his passenger. "We're very near her home; is it all right if we give her a lift?" For the first time that week the bank manager said, "Yes."

Rob's dear old mother clambered into the backseat and they began to make their way to the street where she lived. A few moments passed in silence and then she leaned forward, tapped the banker on the shoulder, pointed at Rob, and said,

"Don't you think he's lovely?" The banker replied, "Very nice indeed, Mrs. Parsons."

So if it is not love that is the greatest gift, what can it possibly be? We are convinced it is acceptance. If a child does not feel accepted by his or her mother, it is almost impossible for the child to feel loved by her.

We hear a great deal these days about "peer pressure" with regard to raising children, and it is true that this dwarfs the power of parental influence for many children, especially in the teenage years. But, in truth, peer pressure is a phenomenon that affects us all: we crave acceptance. What else could make millions of us eat rabbit food, torture ourselves on treadmills, or have plastic surgeons yank, stretch, and redistribute vast areas of our skin so that we look younger? Somebody has convinced us that youth and a certain style of beauty are the things that make us acceptable; and what we want, almost as much as life itself, is to be accepted.

One of the greatest services we can do for our children is to send them into adulthood believing that at least their parents accept them for who they are. In the next section we look at two ways in which children perceive whether or not they really are loved like that.

"I Accept the Way You Look"

One of the greatest pressures on children in modern society is the way they look. Among the most rampant diseases plaguing the young are the eating disorders of anorexia and bulimia. In one study two thousand girls from eleven to eighteen were asked, "What would you most like to change about yourself if you could?" Fifty-nine percent mentioned some aspect of their physical appearance, with only four percent desiring greater ability. In another study children were asked to complete the sentence, "I wish I were . . ." The majority of boys answered, "Taller" and the girls, "Smaller."

We live in a world in which thin is beautiful. In the western world we forget this is a purely cultural phenomenon. A friend of ours went to Uganda. On showing some of the women a photograph of her family, one of them said, "Oh, your mother is beautiful; she is fat just like you." If you've got a moment, browse through a local art gallery. Observe the paintings of women of a few hundred years ago. We guarantee there won't be a size ten in sight, never mind a size six. These were large women—and thought of as beautiful. One woman put it well: "Society always wants women to be the shape it's hardest for us to achieve. In Victorian times when good food was hard to come by, the fashionable shape was 'well-rounded.' Now, with an abundance of foods, not to mention Mars bars, they want us to look like stick insects."

Kids aren't stupid; they know that ugly girls don't get on the front covers of teen magazines or unattractive boys adorn the inside pages. But way before that they have been introduced to the world of "beautiful baby" competitions. One of the saddest sights imaginable must be that of adults who should know better, solemnly gazing into stroller after stroller and judging who is or who is not a "beautiful baby." What, for goodness sake, does a beautiful baby look like? And because of that pressure countless mothers who give birth today will, over the coming weeks, feel disappointed with the way their baby looks. They wanted a cuddly, rounded, rosy-cheeked, smiling angel. What they got looks like a cross between a drowned rat and a prune.

But here's the rub: as that baby grows, she will assess from a million messages—some screamed at her from ads, some whispered in school play-grounds, and most unsaid—whether or not she is "beautiful." Unless that child is destined to be one of the few who meet the standard, she will have to do battle with the world if she is to hold on to her self-esteem. She ought not to have to do battle in the home.

Not far from us lives a very attractive mom. This woman is slim and looks ten years younger than her forty years. Her daughter is seventeen and a little overweight. The other day the mother, in the hearing of some of her daughter's friends, said, "You know, Ceri—I'm forty and I'm in better shape than you." Does that mother love her daughter? Yes, she would probably die for her. Does she accept her? No.

Who Is the Fairest of Them All?

It's amazing how early in life our children imbibe the idea that they must look a certain way to be acceptable. Take, for example, some well-known children's stories. Before you switch off, be assured we do not think we should rewrite every fairy tale to make it politically correct. One of the funniest books published recently takes a sideways swipe at that philosophy. Here's a short example from a politically correct "Red Riding Hood."

> *The wolf said, "You know my dear, it isn't safe for a little girl to walk through these woods alone."*
>
> *Red Riding Hood said, "I find your sexist remark offensive in the extreme, but I will ignore it because of your traditional status as an outcast from society, the stress of which has caused you to develop your own, entirely valid, world view. Now, if you'll excuse me, I must be on my way."*
>
> *Red Riding Hood walked along the main path. But, because his status outside society had freed him from slavish adherence to linear, Western-style thought, the wolf knew a quicker route to Grandma's house . . .*[1]

But having laughed at that, just consider the role of beauty in some of these popular stories and what this may say to our kids. *The Ugly Duckling* is a nice example. At first it looks promising—this little duckling who doesn't fit the mold and is ostracized. So how does our hero get over this? Is it by using other gifts to make his mark or triumphing by sheer personality? No, he does it by . . . becoming beautiful. Inside the ugly duckling is a beautiful swan just waiting to emerge. How many kids have looked in the mirror each morning and wondered how long it will be before their swan shows up?

Or enter the world of Disney and *Snow White and the Seven Dwarfs*. That story has a magic mirror. Not only does this mirror possess incredible powers, it allows you, once in a while, to ask it questions. Think of that. What question would you ask a magic mirror? Well, how about, "Who is the fairest of them all?" We know none of the dwarfs are in the frame, but we needn't have worried, because our tall, slim, dark-haired beauty is ready to help—so long as we can stop her from eating apples.

The list goes on—*Sleeping Beauty, Beauty and the Beast*—but without doubt the best example is *Cinderella*. Look at any child's illustrated book of this timeless story. In the beginning Cinderella looks dirty, unwashed, and her clothes certainly aren't designer. But there is no doubt that this woman is gorgeous. When the fairy godmother comes she doesn't give Cinders a face-lift—this kid doesn't need one—and you can bet your bottom dollar that the handsome prince wasn't bowled off his feet by the horses or the coach, even if he did guess they were actually a bunch of mice and a pumpkin. And who, dare we ask, is the enemy? Well . . . the *ugly* sisters!

Am I Worth Loving?

How do we decide whether we are acceptable and have worth? The answer is that we perceive this from outside ourselves—from others—especially from those we love and respect. What makes life particularly hard is that so often when our self-esteem is at its most vulnerable, our peers are at their most hurtful. What do they sing to us on our special day when we turn eight years old?

> *Happy Birthday to you,*
> *You belong in a zoo,*
> *You look like a monkey,*
> *Happy Birthday to you.*

It's doubtful we'll ever be able to do much to change the cruelty of the very young, but life should be different around our parents. We feel saddencd when we hear parents make derogatory comments, even in a humorous vein, about the physical appearance of their children—especially in front of others.

The other day Dianne complimented a teenager on her new outfit. The girl smiled, but her mother poked a finger at a tummy that was protruding and said, "It'll look even better when she does something about that." Of course a parent will want to help a child who is seriously overweight or counsel a teenager about what he or she can do about that zit on the end of their nose, but somehow we have to let our kids know that we love them anyway. That involves us being manifestly proud of

them when they are at their gawkiest or most awk-
ward, and especially if their particular features don't
happen to fit what society at present calls "attractive." It is so hard for us to get out of the mold. The
other day there was a picture in a newspaper of a
young girl who had tragically lost her life. Rob heard
a mom standing next to him say, "Isn't it tragic, and
she was so pretty." We both understand what she
meant. But it wasn't any more tragic because she was
pretty. It was just tragic.

The truth is that the matter of acceptance is
not just relevant to the child who does not seem very
physically attractive. It is probably even more important for the child who seems the epitome of all that
society calls beautiful. This girl will go through her
life always wondering whether her friends, employers, and the men who say they love her actually just
want her for her looks. That child, as well as her
plainer friend, desperately needs to know that her
mother and father love her for who she is. It not only
will enrich her childhood, but it will come in handy
for that day some years down the road when she asks
the question of the mirror and it says, "Sorry,
honey—not you."

But what of the other issue by which children
decide whether or not their mother really does
accept them?

"I Accept You Regardless of What You Achieve."

The second way that we show our children whether or not they are accepted is by our attitude toward their achievements. One of the most testing aspects of parenthood is finding the balance between motivating our children to reach their potential, without instilling in them the belief that our love for them is conditional on how they perform. As we write, it is halfway through the month of August. For the vast majority of parents this time of year holds no special terrors, but if your child is sixteen or seventeen, the onset of the end of the summer contains trauma unimaginable: it is time for SAT and ACT college entrance exams.

We have long since given up trying to prophesy the results of our children's examinations; in any event it is so much harder with Lloyd. When Katie came home from an examination we used to ask her how she had done. She would produce the test and meticulously take us through each section recalling the way she had answered, and occasionally confessing where she had been stumped. So when Lloyd hit exams we tried the same technique. He came home and we said, "How did math go, son?" He answered, "Fine." This was very encouraging. "Did you bring the paper home so we could look at it?" "No. I lost it on the bus." The next day came and with it another examination. At four o'clock we found ourselves asking, "How was geography?" The oracle again replied, "Fine." And again the paper had disappeared, this time apparently having been set on fire immediately on leaving the school. We asked about all ten subjects and received the decree "fine" to each one. Every parent wants to think the best of their children, and so we spent a blissful two weeks rejoicing that although Lloyd did not seem to have overtaxed himself on studying, his natural flair had obviously come to his aid.

It was not until we saw his report card, which had apparently only narrowly missed the same fate as befell the geography paper, that we both realized that the comment "fine" bore no relation at all to the results achieved. Lloyd had shown a degree of impartiality that would have done credit to a Supreme Court judge. The few successes and the cluster of disappointments had all received the same . . . "fine."

Of course, since then, we have had the opportunity of observing him after many examinations and now understand that when he said "fine" it was actually not in relation to anything at all, least of all the recent test. It was rather a word that loosely interpreted meant, "Here is a little something to keep you quiet until the truth gets out."

We will never forget our going with Lloyd at the age of sixteen to get his GCSE (standardized graduation tests) results. We watched this young man walk across the playground and into the school as we sat in the car and waited. Dianne was, by now, crying, but she wasn't sure why. And suddenly he appeared, results in hand. The comment that came next from his lips seemed strangely unfitting as he was now the proud possessor of a cluster of GCSEs, including English language—"I done real good, Mom!"

We promise you we have tried hard to motivate our children, and who knows whether we've succeeded or not. We're sure that we have gotten lots wrong in this whole area; it's possible to be too easygoing and not push a child hard enough or to push too hard and pressure him or her. But above all we have craved for them to understand that even in the middle of all the yelling, the blackmail, and the forced study-guides for breakfast, they should know for a certainty they were loved—anyway.

The pressure for our kids to achieve can begin at a very young age. This is how one young mom put it:

> *I really enjoy the Mother and Toddler group; it's great for company and a chance to get out of the house, but sometimes I find it a pressure.*
>
> *The moms are all very friendly, but there seems to be a constant comparison of what progress our babies have made. It leaves me feeling inadequate if "everyone else's baby" can sit up without leaning on the sofa, or has started to crawl, or has quite clearly said, "Mommy." Sometimes, though, my baby is the one in front, with most of the others lagging behind, and I feel proud at the achievement.*

Already the other mothers are talking about the best nurseries—and even the best schools. I haven't thought that far ahead, but of course, I realize I must—otherwise all the other children will be reaching heights far above Gemma. There is a baby music and movement group starting up. I must get her name down right away. And I must keep my ears open for any other classes that would aid Gemma's development. It doesn't do to fall behind in this world, and it's never too soon to begin.

Rob remembers visiting a mom who had a six-month-old boy. Rob rang the bell and she yelled, "Come in, the door's open." He entered the hall and hearing some noises coming from the kitchen, made his way there. He will never forget the sight that greeted him. Pamela was kneeling on the floor in front of Toby holding a knife about two inches from his face. She didn't turn round to greet Rob, just shouted over her shoulder, "Grab a chair. I'll be with you in a moment." He sat. She now turned her full attention back to the child, "Toby, this is a knife—a *knife*, Toby—this is a *knife*." The child looked slightly more nonplussed than Rob and seemed more interested in the cat who at this time was devouring Toby's cereal on the kitchen counter.

Eventually the knife was put down, and we had, "Toby, a *fork*—Toby, a *fork*." Rob could see that this mother was utterly committed to working her way through a whole canteen of cutlery and said,

"Look, I'll come back later." "No," she said, "we're just about finished. It's his 'learn a word' hour."

Rob knows it's not always wise to speak your mind in such moments, but he couldn't resist. "What will he do with the word if he learns it? The child can't talk yet." She gave Rob a sympathetic look and said, "Subconscious." He wasn't sure if she was referring to some educational principle or the look on his face, but she went on, "It all goes into their little minds and later it will come popping out."

Fortunately for him, Toby had a more realistic view of life than Pamela and seemed to feel no pressure at all to pop anything out apart from the normal. And it was good for him that he didn't, because in a world where achievement is everything, we can pressure our kids to succeed and, in the process, all but rob them of their childhood.

At home Dianne has a favorite mug; on it is a picture of a harassed mom in one of those minivans that looks like a small bus. She is talking to a solitary young figure next to her: "If Simon's in Cubs, and Helen's in Brownies, and Mark's in Kung-Fu, and Becky's at swimming . . . who the heck are you?"

Of course it's good to give children opportunities, and activities like piano lessons and ballet can be wonderful so long as we don't try to put old heads on young shoulders and, in so doing, make it hard for those kids to just have fun. When they do these things, we need to lighten up a bit. The main aim should be that our kids enjoy playing the piano or learn to love ballet, not end up at the Festival Hall or starring in *Swan Lake* in Moscow.

Sometimes we try to compensate for what we perceive to be our own failures through our children. We want them to do better than we did; we are anxious for them to have the opportunities that we missed. There's nothing wrong with any of that as long as we don't get too messed up about it. Children quickly sense when something is important to us, and they generally want to please, but not every child can win the school races, and even if they manage to, it's an awful burden to believe they've got to go on doing it. Rob was once attacked by an irate father who insisted that his son had beaten Lloyd in a swimming race by a millisecond. If it had been the Atlanta Olympics, we might have gotten excited; but we were on vacation in Cornwall, and it was the small hotel's *Fun* Day.

Just recently we watched a fascinating television program. It was a documentary about beauty queens, except these were nine- and ten-year-olds.

Mothers fussed and primped these prima-donnas who had learned to walk, talk, and ooze sex appeal before they had started their periods. Perhaps one of them will end up as Miss World. We just hope that when they do, and are surrounded by money, success, and glitter, somebody will be able to explain to them where their childhood went.

We send our children into a world that will continually judge them. They will be forced to ask themselves, "Am I clever enough?" "Am I good with people?" "Am I determined/flexible/focused/laid back . . . enough?" And, of course, "Am I attractive enough?" Measuring up to the demands of others is a wearisome business. But we do our children a wonderful service if we send them into that world with an unshakable belief that there is at least one person who, regardless of their grades, weight, or athletic genius, loves them . . . *anyway*. It really is the greatest gift. Most of us, as adults, are still searching for somebody to love us like that.

Where do we find examples of such love? In our experience it is so often among those who parent children with special needs. These parents face the most difficult of circumstances, often with little help or understanding. The charity we work with runs residential weekends for those parents. Some time ago a couple attended who have a Down's syndrome child. The mother said to us, "Our son is twenty-eight years old; in all those years this is the first evening we have ever had away on our own." Those parents do not want anybody to romanticize the task they do; nevertheless in the everyday challenges, in bearing the misunderstanding of others and the knowledge that this is a lifelong commitment, they constantly demonstrate a love that accepts . . . *anyway*.

We recently received a quite remarkable letter from a mother. She had been told that she would never be able to conceive, but eleven years ago gave birth to a daughter. We felt we had to speak to her and had a wonderful conversation: she urged us always to remember those who are the parents of disabled children, for they carry, as she put it, "a responsibility, a love, and a pain that is hard to convey to those who have never been there." This is her story:

> *When my daughter, Kelly, was born, I was told that she was blind, almost certainly intellectually impaired, and with severely dysfunctional internal organs.*
>
> *I will never forget holding this precious child in a shawl and, with tears running down my face, wondering what the future held for her. As I gazed down at her, she looked so vulnerable, and emotion after emotion was flooding through me. I suddenly had a compelling desire to commit my feelings to paper. When she was just seven weeks old, I wrote my daughter a letter. I have kept it in a drawer since the day I wrote it all those years ago. If you think it would help others please use it.*
>
> *April, 11, 1988*
>
> *My darling Kelly,*
>
> *As I write, you are seven weeks old, a very beautiful baby, and unspeakably precious to your father and me. When you were born it was wonderful to have you, a little daughter. Now, with the news that you are blind, we love you with an even more tender love.*

I have wept for you, Kelly, these last days, as I've remembered experiences that you will never have. But I am also deeply sure that all is well and there is nothing to be afraid of in the future.

God's hand is on you and he will shape and fashion you, often through heartache and pain, into an exceptional woman. You are very special to us.

Kelly, I want you to be the best that you can be. Don't ever settle for second best, making your disability an excuse not to be excellent. Be brave and full of laughter. Listen with your ears and your heart to others, always seeking to bring healing and love to them. Be strong and unrelenting in your desire to live life to its fullest. Many precious things will be withheld from you, but the best will always be there for you. Trust God.

My sweet child, I love you so much and I promise to be with you as you grow—in understanding, encouragement, in discipline, and in tenderness.

Your mother,

Elizabeth Thomas

A promise "to be with you as you grow—in understanding, encouragement, discipline, and tenderness." No child could ask more from a mother.

Sixty-Second Wisdom

60 Parenting is a long-haul business. Don't exhaust yourselves in the teenage years; who will they turn to in their forties?

60 Never miss an opportunity to read a story; the day is hurtling toward you when they'll say, "Not tonight, thanks."

60 Don't take all the credit; don't take all the blame.

60 Have a life apart from your kids. If you give yourself completely, they get less.

[Immediately after the birth] nothing had prepared me for the shock of that first meeting. How often, after all, do you meet someone for the first time, already knowing that you will love them passionately? Who was he? Would I like him? Would he like me? I thought him very lovely, but I could not shake off the eerie feeling that he disapproved of me—are you her, are you all?

Kate Saunders writing about her son Felix, in **Sons and Mothers**[2]

Supermom Always . . .

- Has all the stuff to make any school craft project.

- Returns library books several days early.

- Redeems her supermarket coupons before the expiration date.

- Irons her dish towels twice.

- Has neatly plucked eyebrows.

- Knows the school holiday dates.

- Gets to the bottom of the ironing basket.

- Washes gym uniform every Friday night without fail.

Barney, Barney, Barney

Yawning, I make the Barney jigsaw with Joe for the fifth time today. We've read the Barney book at least six times and watched the Barney video twice. Barney is Joe's latest craze. Meanwhile, I am so bored with Barney that I think it possible I might scream very loudly.

I just have to get out of the house at least once today, although I haven't any shopping to do and my friends are either out at work or busy elsewhere. "Let's go to the park," I say cheerfully to Joe. "Want Barney show," says Joe.

I struggle to get Joe into his coat and stroller and push him, protesting, to the nearest park. Once he gets there, of course, he loves every minute. But after his sixth go on the swing and the twelfth turn on the slide, I am so bored with the park that I think it possible I might scream very loudly . . . *indeed!*

I love Joe so much. I really do. It's just that after having a fulfilling career, I'm finding full-time motherhood tedious, and it makes me feel so *guilty.*

Gillian, mother of Joe

CHAPTER FOUR

When a Mother Is Asked "Do You Work?"

or

"If staying at home is so fulfilling, why am I climbing the walls with boredom?"

"If working outside the home is so liberating, why am I permanently shattered?"

Rob says he's glad of the five-year gap between writing *The Sixty-Minute Father* and this book on motherhood. Those years have given him time to talk to thousands of men about the scourge of overbusyness that is killing families. *The Sixty-Minute Father* was written to urge men not to miss spending time with their children, and to encourage them to get involved in their lives. That book was not written out of his success but his failure. Our children are now grown, but when they were small, Rob was often just too busy. I suppose the quote that best sums it up is, "Nobody ever said on their deathbed, 'I wish I'd spent more time at the office.'"

Let Rob give you a taste of what he has been saying to fathers:

A Father Looks Back

A father sat and flipped through a family album. His children were almost adults, and the day when the home was free of untidy bedrooms and blaring music was closer than he wanted. Not an organized album, this one: nobody had, in the suggested manner, written the date and place on the back of each photograph. Eighteen years of home life were randomly thrown together. Yet one could still read in those memories the unmistakable journey this family had made together through the years.

There was a toddler with a broad smile, who showed no hint of embarrassment that he had just one tooth. Two children played on a beach. A shepherd clung grimly to a stuffed lamb in a nativity play that even a kind critic would have described as low budget. There were Christmases, aunts and uncles, and enough animals for a small zoo.

Then the father sighed and reached for a photograph tucked into the sleeve of the album. Smiling out of the photograph was a young man. He stood in what was obviously a hospital room, and in his hands he cradled a newborn baby. This man had built up a business, sat on numerous boards and committees, and had, without a doubt, achieved what some would call success. As he gazed at the photograph, his shoulders sagged. Finally he lifted his head and whispered, "I would trade it all today if I could roll back the years and begin again."

Is he a bad father? Is it that he doesn't care about his children? No, in many ways he is a good father. He loves his family. He provides for them and tries to give them the very best. If you ask him what was most important—his work, his hobbies, or his family—he would answer in a moment, "My wife, my children." Yet he is fifty years old, his children are grown, and he feels he has missed their very childhood.

I understand him so well. When he was small, my son Lloyd used to come into the bathroom in the mornings and say, "Dad, tell me a story while you're shaving." Lloyd asked for those stories every day. Then one day he didn't come. He didn't send me a postcard to warn me this was going to happen. He didn't even say, "By the way, Dad, this morning is the last one." It was simply that on a rainy winter's day at 7:00 A.M., that particular door of childhood silently closed.

Consider those eighteen years of childhood and imagine for a moment the hourglass contains not sand but days. When your child was born, the timer had 6,570 days in it. If your child is ten years old, you have 2,920 left. No amount of money, power, or prestige can increase that number.[3]

Out of Control

Since writing *The Sixty-Minute Father,* Rob is often asked to speak to companies about the challenge of balancing home and work priorities; and increasingly it is mothers who approach him at the end and say something like this, "I understand that you wrote that book for men, but you must know that these are issues that every working mother struggles with." The truth is, we both know it; how could we not? One of the main topics raised by women in their letters to us is the incredible pressure they live under in trying to hold down a job and run a home. Millions of women feel this way because in spite of the fact that more and more fathers are getting involved, the vast proportion of the responsibility of running the home still falls on women. Some mothers express the view to us that they have been "liberated" from the home only to discover a new prison that actually still includes all the old duties with new ones added.

One woman put it like this:

> *People say that being a mom at home is mundane and boring, and I confess that often it was, but am I the only mother who sometimes thinks, "This job is not exactly enthralling—perhaps being tied to the house was not that much worse than being tied to the shop. At least then life was only boring—now it's boring and I'm tearing my hair out."*

The phrase that mothers often use to describe their lives is "out of control." In a recent seminar Rob was giving for business executives he began by asking them when they thought Formula One racing drivers were under the most stress. The normal answers came thick and fast—"On the starting grid," and "When he's passing." Rob shook his head and the delegates went quiet for a moment. Then a woman in the third row said, "When he's pulled into the pits to get refueled and have the tires changed." She was right—for the simple reason that it's the very place where the drivers don't have control. They wait anxiously as others fit the wheels or perhaps lose precious seconds fumbling with the fuel line and finally they roar off to join the fray again.

He could see that large sections of the audience suddenly had a tremendous empathy with the lot of racing drivers. One woman said:

Tell me about it. I have three kids. This morning before 7:00 I had searched for homework done the previous night by my ten-year-old, done the homework for my twelve-year-old, and mopped up where the dog had been sick. The baby-sitter for my toddler was supposed to be at the house at 7:30 A.M. Just as I was about to leave, her mother called to say her daughter had a bad cold and wouldn't be able to come. It was all I could do to stop myself from screaming over the phone, "Bad cold! I'm here about to have a double coronary, and her nose is sniffling?" As long as everything goes according to plan, life is tolerable. But so often it doesn't, and then I lose it.

Enter . . . Supermom!

There is little worse than feeling that life is just out of control. And the problem is that so often society gives us the message that we should be able to cope—easily. Apart from single mothers, who are so often told their children are destined for disaster, working moms are the greatest recipients of guilt in the modern world. And that guilt has two aspects. First there's the worry that they and their kids are missing out because they are not at home; but a little more insidious is the nagging feeling that they should be coping much better with it all. One mom put it like this, "Sometimes I ask myself, 'Am I the only mother who gets home fully intending to cook a decent meal and who ends up throwing a frozen pizza in the oven? Do other mothers who work all day actually fall asleep telling bedtime stories, and find themselves sewing name tags onto gym clothes at midnight?'"

And then, just when we thought life couldn't get any worse, we meet *Supermom.* Supermom not only looks good—she doesn't have lipstick on her teeth, and her skirt is not tucked into the back of her pantyhose—but she balances a demanding job and running the home with clinical efficiency. She really does seem to be able to do it all. This creature is never diverted from her game plan. She bakes, chairs boardroom discussions, and gets to every parent-teacher conference. Her kids never eat pizza for dinner, and she not only doesn't fall asleep reading bedtime stories, in her spare time she also writes them!

The truth is that she's probably not Supermom and in her quieter moments knows it. Anyway, who defined a successful mom as being the cleverest person at time-management or planning? Some of the best moms we know are the most chaotic—their homes, their hair, and their priorities seem a mess. But their kids love them and so, it seems, do all the other kids in the neighborhood.

It's certainly true that mothers have more freedom to work outside the home, and yet many feel trapped by doing so. When we speak to women about this issue they often raise the need for fathers to be more involved in helping in the home and for employers to become more aware of the needs of employees who have children, but almost all agree that it's much deeper than that.

In the following pages we look at two myths that make it hard for mothers to consider these issues dispassionately. One myth demeans the role of the mother at home, and the other, the task of the mother trying to balance dual responsibilities.

Myth Number One:
Looking After Children at Home is Not a "Real Job"

One of the most crucial tasks facing us in a modern society and one to which individuals, the media, and especially government needs to pay heed is that of creating a climate where the task of raising children is seen as a vital and high calling. We must stop degrading the task of bringing up children and, in so doing, making the mother who decides to work part-time, stay at home while her kids are small, or stay at home completely, feel that her brain must have dropped out.

The truth is that some moms whose brains have definitely not dropped out are making the decision to cut back their professional lives in order to spend more time with their families. Julie Akhurt, who resigned the editorship of *Best* for family reasons, said, "The most common reaction I get is, 'How can you give all this up?' which seems to imply that choosing to be a mother is not what you do if you are clever. But I have always known that is what I would do."

Whenever we speak to mothers in our seminars, we find that whether they are moms who work outside the home or moms who stay home looking after small children, nothing gets such a strong reaction as when Dianne relates the reply given by a mom some years ago to the question, "Do you work?" For those of you who have heard it before, forgive us, but here's the whole context of that memorable answer:

> *I remember the evening so well. My husband had been invited to a business dinner and spouses had the privilege of attending as well. For a good week before, I began panicking. My first son was thirteen, and my daughter was three. My second son had just been born; and judging by my*

stomach, large parts of him were still inside. I lay awake at night imagining the other women who would be there. The problem with panic is that it feeds off itself. Most parties I have attended have one woman who looks as if she's stepped off the front cover of Vogue, *but generally the rest of us are an assortment of bodies all trying to make the best of ourselves and not sure if we've managed it. But as I lay awake at night, my mind began to drift, and suddenly all the women in this party were leggy creatures who looked at home on a cat-walk—except for one, who looked like a feature shot from* Wrestling Weekly. *One night I actually slipped out of bed without waking my husband and took a dress downstairs to see if I could get into it. The zipper broke.*

The big moment eventually came and, for some reason, as I entered the room I felt quite confident. Even the sight of two other women in the same dress only threw me slightly, and I caught myself smiling at the sight of the three of us scurrying to different corners of the room. As I passed a mirror, I shot a look at myself; it may have been the lighting, but I thought I looked pretty good. This wasn't going to be so bad after all. And then out of a clear blue sky came a double whammy.

The first of these whammys came in the guise of a lovely lady whom I hadn't seen for ages. She did not intend to hurt me. She is down-to-earth, warm, and caring. She was genuinely pleased to see me and came rushing across. "What a lovely surprise! When's the baby due?" "He's five weeks old," I said. Bless her heart, I thought we'd have to call the paramedics—for both of us!

But it wasn't the worst moment; that came during the meal. I was sitting opposite a very attractive young female executive who after some small talk, leaned forward and asked, "Do you work?"

It's amazing how fast the brain operates. Do I work? *I thought. Well, I knew that the task of motherhood made just about every other job I'd done look easy; I knew that I got up early and went to bed late, and I was sure that three young lives were utterly dependent on me. But did I* work? *I mumbled, "No. I'm just a mom—at home with young children."*

Some years later I related my experience to an older mother who said, "When somebody asks you that again, this is what you must say . . ." I went home and practiced it, and five months later, as I stood in a crowded room with a piece of cheese on the end of a stick, some poor soul asked me again, "Do you work, Karen?"

"Yes," I replied. "I'm in a program of social development. At present I'm working with three age groups. First, with babies and toddlers. That involves a basic grasp of medicine and child psychology. Next, I'm working with teenagers. I confess the program is not going too well in that area.

Finally, on evenings and weekends I work with a man, age thirty-nine, who's exhibiting all the classic symptoms of midlife crisis. That's mainly psychiatric work. The whole job involves planning, a 'make it happen' attitude, and the ability to crisis-manage. I used to be an international fashion model, but I got bored."

Yes!!!

Myth Number Two: Balancing Home and Work Is Just a Matter of Organization

The heart of this delusion is that any mother worth her salt should be able to cope with raising small children, doing a full-time job, cooking their meals, washing their clothes, helping with their homework, reading them stories, and still have enough energy left to be a sexual athlete. One mother put it like this, "If all this is so easy, why aren't men doing it? He wants me to do all this stuff and still be what he calls, 'great in bed.' I said to him, 'I'm exhausted. You know when I'm great in bed? When I'm asleep.'"

Many mothers feel pressured when they read that "You can have it all"—a busy career, a fulfilling family life, and lots of social life as well. But the problem is that no matter how many time-management courses we attend and no matter how many day-planners we possess, the one thing we can't change is the amount of time we each have. Every day comes to us full of 86,400 seconds. It doesn't much matter whether we're the president of the company or the receptionist, we get the same; every day we spend it all and start the next day with another 86,400 seconds. And that means we have to choose. An old Eastern proverb says, "If you do this, you can't do that."

But sometimes we slip into a lifestyle in which we try to "do it all." A mom said to us recently:

> *I was just driving myself into the ground. John and I were like ships passing in the night and the things that should have been bringing me pleasure, like my son's soccer games after school, were just an added pressure. One night we sat down and talked about it. We decided I would reduce my hours to be there when the kids got in from school and we'd move to a smaller house and reduce our mortgage. I just wanted us to start living again before it was too late.*

Another mom wrote:

> *I don't know how it happened, but we just got used to an extra income for things like a second vacation and meals out. When I realized I was practically having a nervous breakdown and missing my kids growing up, for the sake of two weeks in Hawaii and a couple of dinners, I sat down and cried and then laughed. I still work but nothing like those old hours.*

Somebody has said that motherhood is "guilt-edged insecurity." But most moms don't need more guilt. Susan is a mom of two small children age three and five. She doesn't go to work to chase unnecessary money. She works so her family can make ends meet. She doesn't need more guilt; she needs more support—support that will allow her to make choices that are best for her and her children, choices that will help her enjoy, instead of just enduring, her motherhood. It's the right of every mother.

The Lure of the Illusions

And, finally, as we come to the close of this section, Rob already mentioned that when our kids were small he made many mistakes in terms of overcommitment. He has spent years talking to fathers about three illusions that kept him in that lifestyle far longer than he should have been. We don't presume they will be relevant to your situation, but they just might be.

The first illusion was that Rob used to say to himself, "I'm doing this for them; I want them to have more than I had." It may be a noble sentiment; the problem with it is that most kids would far prefer fewer "things" and more of us. One child psychologist put it well: "We are so busy giving our kids what we didn't have, we don't have time to give them what we *did* have."

The second illusion was that life would not always be so busy. Rob would tell himself that this pressurized period would soon pass and then he would have more time for the things that really mattered. The truth is that for most of us this is not a busy period; this is life. Until we realize this, we'll be forever putting off things that really matter to us with the promise that there will be time . . . tomorrow.

And the third illusion was that the door of childhood would be open forever. Rob believed that when he said to the kids, "later" or "we'll do it next weekend," that there always would be a "later." But there comes a time when they don't really want to do things with us. They still love us, but if we think that chances to tell stories and play board games will last forever, we may be kidding ourselves.

But let the final words on this whole issue go to a working mother. Her name is Mary Bourgoin.

> *These days it seems that my city is one of weary women, or, more accurately, exhausted working mothers. For several months I have been among those who rise at dawn to shower, blow-dry their hair, pack lunches, do a load of washing, iron a few shirts, and glance at the morning paper to make sure the world is not ending before 9:00 A.M.*
>
> *Provided there is no last-minute scramble for missing shoes or homework, and the hamster isn't lost, my three daughters are at school by 8:40 A.M., and I am on my way to the "real world."*
>
> *My job is interesting: working on Capitol Hill as a journalist, investigating the legal process, interviewing members of Congress—all described*

in my old school magazine under the heading, "Mary Bourgoin's Glamorous Job!" The only problem is that most of the time I feel that I have one foot on a banana peel and the other on ice.

Balancing marriage, motherhood, and career has become the classic women's problem of modern life. For those who can pull it all together, life is a first-class act. But judging from my own experience and from talking with other women, life is often a constant round of heartburn, ulcers, and anxiety attacks.

During the past decade more and more women have entered the labor force. Although much discussion about career opportunities for women focuses on personal growth and fulfillment, the fact is that the majority of women work because they need the money.

Yet it seems that my generation has now romanticized careers as the cure-all for identity crisis, the supermom syndrome, the housewife blues, and the empty-nest heartache. Replacing the happy housewife heroine is the successful business woman who climbs up the corporate ladder without chipping her nail polish, who breezes through the day wearing immaculately tailored clothes, and who returns home, hairdo intact, to an adoring husband and two well-adjusted children.

The sad and obvious truth is that a great many women are now finding out what men have always known: dead-end jobs abound; most work eventually becomes boring; bosses, colleagues, and clients can be demanding, irritating, and nasty; and it is just as easy to feel trapped and unhappy sitting in a posh office amid the trappings of success as it is standing in the kitchen surrounded by whining preschoolers.

The truth is that the breezy you-can-do-it-all articles leave out an important factor—energy. "Motherhood," as somebody has said, "saps the energy." And so does a high-pressure career where upward job mobility is a way of life.

Marriage is also demanding, requiring inner strength and motivation to keep a relationship from going stale. Simply put, when it comes to energy, physical or emotional, we have only so much.

I am weary of magazine articles about the successful dynamic mother-wife career wonder-woman. Something is missing. The unglamorous parts are airbrushed out. The stories bear no relation to reality.

The tales I hear from women—conversations on the subway, concerns over coffee, instructions whispered over the phone to children, husbands, baby-sitters, teachers—describe the edited-out scenes: sick children sent to school or left home alone; baby-sitters who permit their charges to watch endless hours of television; sleeping babies who are awakened at 6:00 A.M. and delivered to day care centers at 7:00 A.M.; the growing number of latchkey children—eight- and nine-year-olds who are left unsupervised on their own after school until a parent returns home; the endless makeshift arrangements for the dreaded school holidays, teacher in-service days, and schools closed because of snow.

My mother was poor; she was a seamstress in a shirt factory. She knew all too well the reality of the world of working mothers. "Work," my mother often says watching from the sidelines as I try successive variations of my marriage-career-children juggling act, "is terribly overrated."

One recent evening on my way home from work, bone tired, worried about my equally busy husband, a melancholy daughter, and a cantankerous boss, I came across a newspaper article about several celebrity women.

"It's nifty," said one, "that women are no longer bound by traditional role models and careers." Yes, I agreed, and yet I had the feeling that she was naively enthusiastic about the "new woman" viewing the world through the wrong end of the binoculars. When one panelist described how she manages to do it all, my doubts turned to convictions. She said, "My husband and I both work at home. We have a year-old child whose care is shared equally between the two of us and a nurse."

I was too tired to laugh.[4]

It's almost impossible to be able to discuss these issues without being polarized either as somebody who wants to release women from the ties of home-making or as somebody who wants to tighten the knots. The truth is that now women are increasingly able to pursue work outside the home, the responsibility of giving support to those who make that choice involves us all—spouses, employers, and government. But the only sensible way to do that is against a background where the task of staying at home to care for children is given dignity, and those who make that choice are given the support they need as well.

Above all we need to remember the proverb mentioned above: "If you do this, you can't do that." Life may not be quite as "modern" as we think. Although much in society has changed, life still comes with more or less the same package of responsibilities as it always did: our relationships need time and attention, as do the kids; the food needs to be bought and cooked; the rent or mortgage needs to be paid; and we need to find a little time to reproduce.

The issue of whether to work outside the home, and if so how much, and how to split responsibilities between spouses is not easy to resolve. For many there will be no choice. But whatever you decide, don't be plagued by what others think. Do what you consider right for you and your family. But don't be too tired to laugh.

Sixty-Second Wisdom

(from a mother of four)

When your pregnancy test turns blue remember:

60 You've got nine months to get used to the idea.

60 At least you'll get a seat on the bus.

60 It'll be the baby's first time too—you can learn together.

60 You can eat king-size Mars bars—how will anyone know?

Things Mothers Say . . .

- I wish someone had told me that glowing mother love is not automatically delivered with the baby and you don't feel like the mom on the baby food ad who has time to roll around on a white bedspread in her size four jeans with a peaceful, gurgling baby. You feel tired, sore, frightened, and completely overwhelmed by responsibility hormones. You fight with your husband more than ever. And I wish someone had said that all this is normal.

- You have to be there for them. Whatever they do, wherever they go, even if they've really hurt you—you still have to be there for them.

- You never stop being a mother. When they've grown up and left home, you have no authority over them at all and you can't do anything about it when they make mistakes. You just have to let them go; but when they leave, part of you goes with them.

You're Not the Only Mother Who . . .

- Spends three hours and the entire weekly food budget on a really special meal for them all, only to have it greeted with questions like, "What's this green stuff?" and "Can I have cheese on toast?" And you lock yourself in the bathroom, wipe away a tear, and ask yourself why it matters so much, and why it hurts so much. But you never quite know.

- Says, "If ever I leave home, it will surely be at a quarter past five."

- Climbs into one of their empty beds at three in the morning because they've all climbed into yours when they got scared in the night. You've heard all the advice about settling them back into their beds so they'll know there's nothing to fear, but you've already spent half the night with your head leaning on the bedside table. That two-foot, six-inch bed with the Beatrix Potter duvet looks just fine.

Anxious Mom

I walked painfully into the house while Mark lifted the baby seat out of the car and carried it into the sitting room. I gazed down at my sleeping newborn son, hoping the sniffly sound in his nose wasn't anything to worry about. There were no nurses to ask now—we'd brought him home from the hospital after just two days, and it was up to us to get it right.

I didn't get much sleep that night—not that Sam kept me awake. He only woke once. But I had to keep looking at him, putting a hand on his back to feel his body rise and fall, checking to be sure he was still breathing.

I lost count of the times I took Sam to the clinic or the doctor, or requested late-night advice in the first year of his life. It was only when I had my second baby, Beth, three years later, that I realized how much I'd worried. I even had to be reminded to take Beth to the doctor for checkups. I feel embarrassed now as I remember my anxiety over Sam—but I knew the medical profession was used to it and didn't mind. "Another first-time mother," they probably said to each other.

CHAPTER FIVE

When a Mother Is Alone

Some years ago Rob was invited to take part in a seminar on relationships in the family. It was the coffee break, he was the next speaker, and he was sitting on the edge of the stage waiting for his turn. Suddenly a woman approached him; she was about thirty-five years old, and had obviously been crying. She sat next to him and he asked her what was wrong.

She explained that the previous speaker had stressed the importance of a father in the life of a child. She turned to Rob and said, "My children, a boy and a girl, have no father; he left years ago. Are they destined to fail? My son is causing me a lot of worry at the moment." Rob felt tremendous compassion for her.

Nobody believes more strongly than us that, if possible, it's best for a child to have a mother and a father. But it's sad if, in making that basic point, we make single parents not only feel second-class but suggest they are doomed to failure. Rob listened for a while then said, "I don't know you, but you sound like a fantastic mother; your kids are fortunate; don't believe for another second that they are certain to fail." He gave her the number of an organization that works to help and support single parents and said, "You *will* make it."

A month later Rob got a letter:

Thank you so much for the time you spent with me. You will never know what it meant to me. You gave me hope. I took notes of some of the things you said in your talk and when I got back I made a short presentation to a parenting group in my church. I have never spoken in public before and I was so nervous, but halfway through I looked up and saw my fifteen-year-old son standing at the back listening. When it was over, he came straight up to me, put his arms around me and said, "Mom, you were fantastic!"

These days we never begin one of our seminars without specifically welcoming those who are single parents. We believe they have the hardest job on the face of the earth. A friend of ours who is a single-parent mom overheard another mother talking about people like her: "I've got no time for single parents. They're a problem; their children are trouble. It's their own fault anyway. They have children by different fathers and expect us to keep them." The reality is far from that. The latest statistics show that less than 10 percent of single mothers are under the age of twenty. Sixty percent have been married and 9 percent are fathers. There are many kinds of single parents: some have experienced the death of a spouse; others have known divorce or desertion. Some have gone ahead with a pregnancy knowing almost from day one there would never be a father's presence and support. Some single parents—usually mothers—have custody of their children; others may see them on weekends only. Many have known unimaginable hurt. One mother wrote telling us what life had been like for her and her children.

> *Over the years there were repeated affairs, use of pornography, violence, control, etc. In between each crisis he was a different man. He lived a Jekyll and Hyde existence, and the children suffered because they never knew who he was. Since he left, my daughter has told me she used to brace herself as she walked downstairs every morning and was so relieved if he was "nice" daddy. The only thing she has questioned was why I didn't ask him to go years ago. She has been so hurt. "Why can't I have a daddy like other girls?" she asked once. "And I don't mean Dad; he's never been a Daddy to me."*

We spoke to the mother who wrote that letter. She told us that of course she wanted her children to have a father who loved them and cared for them. But that wasn't an option for them; survival was.

Carole is another typical example of somebody who honestly believed that single parenthood would never be an issue for her. She had been married for five years and was eight months pregnant when her husband, Paul, left her for the woman he had been having an affair with for the previous two months. We have no idea what attitude Carole had toward single-parent moms before this trauma hit her, but she summed up what so many face when, just before the birth of her baby, she said, "All the joy of having this child is gone. He won't be there when the baby is born. There will be lots of other issues too—like leaving the baby at home because I'll have to work to pay the mortgage. I'm just not sure I can do it all alone."

And every single-parent mom or dad will have heard through the media what research has shown with regard to their children's behavior and prospects: without doubt it is better for a child to have a mother and a father. But what so often doesn't come across is the tenacity, sheer dedication, and hope that most single parents have. The single parent often has to do battle on half a dozen fronts at once. Although she knows she can't do it, she is trying to be both a mother and a father to this child.

Money is often tight, but the real bottom line is that you face issues big and small—alone. It doesn't matter whether it's a blocked sink, a teenager experimenting with drugs, a car with a dead battery, or a lump in the breast. You have to somehow deal with it—yourself. But added to that, and perhaps worst of all, is that you don't know whether the difficulties you are experiencing are the normal ones that every mother is going through, or whether it really is because your child doesn't have a father. At times you are fit to burst; you spend half your life worrying about what's happened and the other half worrying about what might happen.

A couple of years ago Dianne was away and Rob was holding down the fort. Lloyd was usually pretty good about getting in on time, but on this occasion he was due to be in by midnight and there was no sign of him. It's a scenario that every parent of teenagers understands completely. At about 12:05 Rob started to panic. At 12:15 he made a cup of tea and told himself not to be stupid. At 12:25 he thought, *This is common; think what you were like when you were young.* That really panicked him. At 12:45 he started rifling drawers for Lloyd's friends' telephone numbers. At 12:50 he descended into a spiral of panic from which there was no escape. He was sure that the sirens he could hear in the distance were on top of ambulances conveying our son to the hospital or that any moment he would see a blue light flash in the street outside.

When Lloyd eventually came in, Rob didn't know whether to hug him or ground him until his late forties. And then he realized that this is what single parents go through every day of the week. It's not that there aren't friends and family who care; it's just that in the everyday business of parenting, whatever they face, they face alone.

One single-parent mom summarized the difficulties:

Twenty-four-hour parenting

There's no one else when you've just had enough. Even ordinary things can seem like mountains to climb. I'm scared of getting the flu because somebody has to care for my kids. The other day I had to go into the hospital for a minor operation, but first I had to get somebody to keep my two children for a couple of days. You'd think it would be easy, but sometimes it seems impossible.

Pain

At the same time as trying to be Supermom you are trying to cope with the terrible pain of being left alone—a whole bundle of emotions—anger, grief, rejection—and sometimes sheer bewilderment. The worst part is when the kids say, "If daddy had loved us, he wouldn't have left."

Money

It's often hand-to-mouth. I work outside the home part-time but even so we don't have much. I don't care so much about myself, but I want them to have what other kids have.

There's just nobody to talk to . . .

Nobody to say, "Don't be silly," or "Let the baby cry for a while," or "You're doing a great job." I so often have the sense that I really am on my own.

Lynda Hunter, who is a single-parent mom with three children, wrote to us and shared some of the lessons she had learned.

The other day I forgot that my daughter had to stay after school for a drama rehearsal, and I spent the best part of an hour waiting for her out-side her school. As I sat in the car on that warm August afternoon, my mind went back fourteen years when, while paying bills, I found an unusu-ally large hotel receipt from a business trip my hus-band had taken. I called the hotel for an explanation. Their reply changed my life forever: my husband was having an affair. When I con-fronted him, he simply walked away from our mar-riage, notwithstanding the fact that both our girls were under three, and I was pregnant with our son.

The next few months became a blur as the baby came and I was served with divorce papers. For some reason I can't understand, I felt ashamed, and for reasons I can understand, completely bro-ken. The only thing I wanted to do was to hide in the house and let the world pass me by. And then one day I saw my son roll over in his bed for the first time. It struck me that his young life was already afflicted with heartache, but he didn't know that and he was just getting on with mak-ing progress. How could I do any less?

As I sat in the car, fourteen years later, I asked myself, "What helped me get on with the business of living? What lessons have I learned as a single mother?"

The first is the most profound and was the most difficult to learn: I could not be a father to my children; I could only be the best mother I could possibly be. We all want the best for our children, and so many of us single parents feel we must compensate for the loss of a father. But we can only do so much. You just can't be mom and dad. One way I have gotten over that is to welcome the involvement of men that I trust in my children's lives. Of course these are normally professionals—it could be a teacher, a youth leader, or a sports coach. The alternative is to reinforce the belief that because one man has let us down, there are no good ones out there. I don't believe it and more important I don't want them to believe it. I welcome any help that I can trust in the task of bringing up these kids.

I also discovered that sometimes I didn't get help because I didn't ask for it. I am very independent and, to be honest, I felt enough of a failure already. But I discovered that if I made my needs known other people would help: they would pick up the kids from school occasionally; dads who lived nearby would make sure to include my son when they took their kids to soccer games; friends would occasionally baby-sit so I could get a break. But if I didn't ask, people assumed I was doing all right.

Perhaps the biggest thing is that I shook off the guilt. I did all I could to keep my marriage from falling apart. Sure I'd made mistakes, but I couldn't bear total responsibility—that would crush me. I had somehow, for my kids' sake, tried to put the past behind me and live each day as it came. Part of that, for me, was forgiveness. I know it sounds strange, but one day I sat in the kitchen and wrote down every hurtful thing my husband had ever done to me. I held the list in my hands and cried, and then I asked God to help me forgive. When I was done, I burned the paper. Of course I still remember those hurts, but somehow I feel free of my ex-husband's power over me. I have tried to forgive him and in the process somehow got free myself. I never criticize him to the kids—he is still their father—turning them against him won't help me or them.

Then I concentrated on the positives. My kids have a mother who loves them and who wants to spend time with them. I know from watching the busy lives of some two-parent families that my kids get more of my time than many of their friends do from their parents. Single parenthood focuses you. I'm not working to get the latest car. I'm working as little as I can to make ends meet and when I'm not working I'm with those kids.

I accepted the fact that I am not the perfect mother, and even more, that many of the issues I went through with my children—whether it was a toddler having tantrums, a child who hated school, or a teenager who's giving everybody a hard time—are normal. Almost every mother, single-parent or not, faces these things. In other words I stopped beating myself up for no good reason.

And finally I learned that, although money was almost always tight, most children prefer a parent's time to expensive toys. I couldn't give my kids the latest computers, bikes, or televisions in their bedroom, so I had to find ways to somehow make up for that. We discovered that doing simple things together—learning to cook, putting up a tent in the yard, sometimes even bargain hunting in second-hand shops, was a lot more fun that sitting in front of a computer. Above all, my children and I learned to laugh together. I have wonderful kids. That doesn't stop them from being kids, driving me crazy with worry at times, but our trouble has brought us close. We are there for one another.

As I was still trundling back through the years, my seventeen-year-old daughter tapped on the car window and jerked me back to reality. She said, "You were miles away, Mom."

I gazed at her and thought, It has turned out better than I dared hope. But you will never know, at times, how very hard it's been.

"Oh," I said, "I was just reminiscing."

"Well, don't," she replied. "What's for dinner?"

Sixty-Second Wisdom

Understand teenspeak . . .

60 You say: "You look nice, dear."
She thinks: *"I must look uncool! I'll change."*

60 You say: "He's a nice boy."
She thinks: *"How can I dump him kindly?"*

60 You say: "Have you got enough money?"
She thinks: *"Has Ivana Trump?"*

60 You say: "Get home at a sensible time."
She thinks: *"Six A.M.'s sensible for milkmen."*

Why Did I Worry?

Why did I worry that he should be first to:
sleep through the night
point to his nose
say "Hello, Dad"
eat with a fork
sleep in a bed
sign his name
learn the piano?

When at seventeen he:

sleeps through the day
pierces his nose
grunts at his dad
eats with his fingers
sleeps on the floor
calls himself Zog
plays the bongo.

Why was I anxious that he wouldn't:

tell the time
learn to swim
get to make friends
cross the road safely
learn the value of money
be attractive to girls
want to know me?

When at seventeen he:

is always in at 2 A.M.
spends every summer Saturday at the beach
has an address book as thick as a
telephone directory
is off to India this summer
earns more than I do at his part-time job
appears to have a harem
still (occasionally) gives me a hug.

Mothers' Race

Watching the lineup for the mothers' race on field day is a good way of reminding yourself of the diversity of motherhood style. There are usually one or two "Competitive Carlas." They've been training for weeks under cover of darkness, and they intend to WIN. Just the same way they expect their kids to . . . every time.

Next to them you'll see "Slap-Dash Sophie." She'll run in her shoes with her skirt hitched up (her child's the one with his hands over his face). She'll run happily along and probably arrive last without making too much effort and doesn't really care what anyone thinks.

Then there's "Tell-Them-How-To-Do-It Tina." She misses the starting gun because she's busy telling the next two in the line how to run the race. When she gets to the end in tenth place, it's someone else's fault, and she'll talk about the unfairness of the race all the way home.

"Keeping-Up-Appearances Kerry" runs because she wants to be seen doing the "right thing." She's desperate to get on the PTA committee, but her anxious expression, shared by all three of her children, tends to make other moms wary of her. She will genuinely lose sleep if she is placed further down the rank than third.

"All-Right-Then Ann" is the one who was persuaded to join in by her two boys against her better judgment. She hardly ever runs—let alone in a straight line—but she doesn't want to let them down. She throws her shoes into the long jump pit just before the race and will probably lose them, but who cares; this is for the expression on those two faces! She runs as fast as she knows how and is genuinely surprised to find herself in second place. Her triumph earns much laughter at the supper table.

Perhaps Ann's the only one who takes time to find comparisons between the race today and the mothering she does. *It's all over too quickly,* she thinks. There are no real winners or losers, and training doesn't make much difference. You just have to get on and do it the best way you can, in your own style, and watch the expressions on those little faces. And, above all, hope with all your heart that just as "Competitive Carla" is about to break the tape, she trips and goes headlong into the concession stand.

Shopping

I am in my late forties and took my daughter, age fourteen, to get myself a new outfit for a wedding. You know what it's like; I had trudged around store after store, but finally I found something I thought was really nice. As I slipped into it in the changing room, I felt really good. I emerged to get my daughter's verdict. She looked up from her magazine and said, "No, it's too young for your face."

You're Not the Only Mother Who . . .

. . . when your second baby arrives, abandons all those great ideals you had with the first:

- Didn't let the first one suck his fingers, let alone the cat's tail.

- Gave the first one organic baby rice; this one survives on peanut butter on toast.

- Changed the first if he dribbled down his bib; this poor kid looks like an extra on *Oliver Twist.*

CHAPTER SIX

When a Mother Is Sick

Wendy Bray

Just before Wendy began helping us with this book, she discovered she had cancer. Most mothers will not experience what she is going through but, nevertheless, difficult times hit us all. Though this is the shortest chapter in the book, it may well contain the deepest lessons.

When each of my two children were born, I looked down at their pink wrinkled faces in the knowledge that I was their Mom—that I would always love them, care for them, and protect them, to the best of my ability. It seemed a certainty, a right, a privilege. When, earlier this year, I was diagnosed with an advanced aggressive cancer, everything changed. The certainty of my care was shaken. The right to be there for them was suddenly removed, and the privilege of mothering them grew to incredible proportions. Now I have to consider that although there is a strong possibility that I *will* carry on mothering them, that I *will* be there for them in six months, two years, ten years, there is an equally strong possibility that I *will not,* that I will die as my son starts high school and my daughter moves further into her teenage years. That I won't be around just at the time when, in many ways, they will need me most, leaving my husband, family, and friends to guide them through those difficult years without me.

Suddenly even the mistakes I've made as a mom seem precious as I realize that the "rights" and "certainties" of motherhood were probably never there anyway, just the privileges and responsibilities.

It is as if "normal motherhood," if there is such a thing, is Plan A, but I have to find a Plan B. The insurance backup. The contingency plan. Plan B is impossible to find because there is no insurance policy for a mother's love. All I can do is build in them the resources, the skills, the faith, the love, and simple wisdom they will need to live. With or without me. Love them and laugh with them now in the hope that I can go on loving and laughing with them.

For now at least, I am not afraid of the cancer. I am not afraid of death. I know that all of us as a family are in the palm of God's hand. He knows what I *am* afraid of. It's when, in my imagination, I can hear the children calling for me in the distance just as they have many times over the past thirteen years. Their calling "Mom" has become like a familiar tune with many variations—calling for attention, calling for help, calling to ask if dinner is ready or to share a joke. But in this dream they keep on calling. Their cries become more and more desperate, wondering why I'm not responding. But I can't get there.

Somebody else has to go and comfort them and tell them that Mom can't come. Until they understand that Mom never *will* come. Then there is the empty, overwhelming feeling that breaks my heart that I have let them down.

How would I have responded as I held those two newborns if somebody had told me about that dream? Would I have handed them back? Said I'd changed my mind? Demanded a rewrite of the story? No. Because we are called to mother whatever the circumstances. We only have to watch the news to understand how many are mothering "against the odds" at the risk of great pain.

I don't think the experience of the last months has made me value the children more or take them less for granted as might be expected. Perhaps I was already aware of the brevity of their childhood. But it *has* made me realize that there is a hidden quality of love enveloped in difficult circumstances of which only a few will have a privileged glimpse. A kind of velvet lining to a broken vessel that infuses the day-to-day with something special.

Mothering is all about facing the pain and mothering *anyway*. Loving anyway, laughing *anyway*. And thankfully, there is still more than enough to laugh at. I still look down at their pink wrinkled faces—when they're giggling. In all the sadness and seriousness of the issues we're facing, the giggling never stops. Who would want it to!

CHAPTER SEVEN

When a Mother Feels Guilty

Motherhood is a risky business because mothers get blamed for the ills of the world. Even when, by any standards, these women have given love and commitment until it is coming out of their ears, somebody is always near at hand to point out the deficiency in potty training, discipline, or education that has ruined their kids' lives. These mothers are either too laid back or overpossessive; they have robbed their kids of their time by going out to work or bored them to death by staying at home; they left teaching them to read too late or killed their love of books by pushing them too young; and if they hadn't skipped pages when they used to read those bedtime stories, this child would have passed English.

It's hard to take that kind of pressure without it getting to you. As we talk to mothers, we find that time and time again the same word keeps coming up—*guilt*. All sorts of moms—young ones, old ones, stay-at-home, out-to-work, and single moms—say the same thing. Typical comments are:

- I've lost confidence in my ability to parent.
- It's too late to go back and put it right.
- I'm overwhelmed by the responsibility of it all.

One mother summed it all up:

> *It's a disease prevalent among mothers. You'll recog-*
> *nize the symptoms when you hear phrases such as:*
> *"I'm sorry but . . ." or "I know I ought to but . . ."*
> *If you ask a mother if she goes out to work, she*
> *might reply: "No, I'm only a housewife and*
> *mother," or perhaps: "Yes, I do—but it's only part-*
> *time, and she really loves going to daycare, and I'm*
> *always back for bedtime, and we have quality time*
> *together when I'm not at work. . . ."*
>
> *The disease is called guilt. We sufferers feel the*
> *need to justify ourselves to others, to apologize for*
> *our actions, and constantly to compare our own*
> *shortcomings to those of other people. It starts*
> *when you're a mom-to-be. You feel you shouldn't*
> *have run for the bus or painted the bedroom ceil-*
> *ing on your own—because it might be bad for the*
> *baby. But the guilt reaches its antenatal height in*
> *the delivery room. You should be able to manage*
> *without an epidural; on no account should you*
> *have a Caesarean.*
>
> *After the birth it gets worse. Your baby is the*
> *only one in the hospital who cries through the*
> *night and keeps everyone else awake. You know*
> *you ought to breast-feed like everyone else, but you*
> *simply can't. You must have your shower and be*
> *dressed before the nurse educator arrives at*
> *10:00 A.M.*
>
> *And so it goes on. The guilt grows with the*
> *child, reaching peaks when everybody else's child is*

potty trained first and seems to reach all the other milestones earlier too. You should have put her name down earlier for that really good school; now her whole future career is spoiled because you were too late. You should have been there for sports day—even though it was your grandmother's funeral that afternoon. You should have noticed that this wasn't just teenage angst and wanting time off school; it was actually mononucleosis.

You're guilty because you leave your child and go out to work while the woman next door is an at-home mom. What you don't realize is that the woman next door is feeling guilty because she isn't contributing to the family income and because she is "only" a housewife, and she's feeling inadequate because she watches how well you cope with career and family!

Why can't we decide what's right for us as a family and go ahead and do it—whether it's breast-feeding, going back to work, moving, having another child—without worrying so much? Answer: because we're mothers, and motherhood goes with guilt like a horse with a carriage.

We're tempted to say, for the sake of equality, that guilt also affects many fathers; but in our experience this is often much later—usually when they look back after their children are grown and perhaps wish they had been more involved. For many women, however, mother-guilt becomes a way of life. This shouldn't be too surprising; modern mothers face special pressures that can easily lead to a sense of failure:

Pressure Number One: Expectations

As we look back on our own childhoods we have no doubt that we had good parents, but it may just be that the parenthood examination was a little easier then. Rob says he can't remember his father reading him bedtime stories or spending vast amounts of time with him or speaking to him about his future or his love life or teaching him woodworking. Was his father a good disciplinarian? The answer is hard to give, because for some reason that is not now immediately apparent, his children obeyed him without question. Rob's father not only rarely spanked them; he rarely shouted. In fact if he lifted his eyebrow over the newspaper, you knew you were in a lot of trouble. Did they have a close relationship with him? Probably not. Did he love them? Certainly, although he rarely told them so.

So how come Rob can look back and say, "He was a good father"? The answer is, "Because the expectations were different then." He saw his role as that of the breadwinner and the disciplinarian. He worked for fifty years and in all that time had only eleven days off due to sickness. There was always food on the table and clothes on our back.

Did Rob's father ever feel guilty as a parent? Of course we don't really know, but Rob says he would be staggered to discover that his father even thought about it. His mother worked hard both inside and outside the home and showered her children with affection. Did she ever feel guilty? Again, Rob doubts it—perhaps only that they didn't have as much in terms of material possessions as other kids.

How different for today's parents. We live in a world where we are used to seeing pop stars, football players, and mass murderers lay the blame for any difficulties they encounter at the feet of their parents. We begin to imagine our children on some morning television talk show spilling the beans about us. It's not difficult to be worried. We look at other families and we are sure their children are more polite, have tidier bedrooms, and do their homework more diligently than ours. And then fear takes over. Our mind begins to run away with us and we think, *Today it's just a late homework assignment, but he'll probably fail all his exams, he doesn't eat properly, his bedroom is a mess, he is going to ruin his life.*

If we don't do something to halt these runaway fears they can immobilize us. This is so because we begin to lose confidence in our parenting. We are constantly saying to ourselves things like, "I dealt with that badly" or "I've blown it again" or "If I hadn't lent her the money to go out she'd never have met that dreadful boy." Even worse, we begin to see those events as irretrievable—the damage is done—forever. The truth is, we do blow it as parents and we do deal with things badly, but we're learning on the job as well.

The real killer is when we come to believe that parents who get it right (whatever that is) would have dealt with a situation in a certain way. Imagine that your fifteen-year-old daughter was meant to be home at eleven-thirty and she rolls in at one o'clock. You say to her, "You're grounded for a month." She yells, spits, and says she hates you. And the following day, while shopping, you meet a mother who seems to have perfect children who says, "Oh, no, I would never do that. This is what you should have said to her: 'You are almost an adult, and I am being unreasonable. Could we agree to twelve o'clock next time?'" As you walk away, you notice you are talking to yourself, "She's right: I blew it; I should have reasoned with her."

And at that very moment you meet Cathy, who everybody knows has a Ph.D. in motherhood. She shakes her head when she hears the advice suggested by the first woman and whispers in your ear, "The key is in the spending money. Tell your daughter that next time you'll deduct one dollar for every ten minutes that she's late." You thank her profusely and rush off dying to try it, until you suddenly have a vision of your daughter coming in at two-thirty in the morning, handing you twenty-four dollars and saying, "That should cover it, Mom."

Your head is whirling. What should you do? The answer is that you should probably go with your original instincts. You know your daughter better than anybody else. The reality is that most "solutions" have to be changed, adapted, or renegotiated as the years go by. If one strategy doesn't work, try something else. We must somehow stop the guilt, caused by unrealistic expectations, that can rob us of the confidence to parent our children.

Pressure Number Two: Isolation

Dianne has an inspirational poster on our kitchen wall. Having said that, it's not your normal run-of-the-mill affair; you know the sort of thing—"Today is the first day of the rest of your life." She used to have that hanging there and then one evening, when she was standing ankle-deep in water because the washing machine had died, with five chicken fingers nicely on fire in the frying pan, and Lloyd telling her he'd lost the hamster, she apparently thought, *No, if the rest is like the first day, you can keep it.* Lots of her inspirational posters have been trashed around dinnertime, but one has remained.

Dianne is sure the artist didn't intend it to lift mothers' spirits or help them to face another day, but this is what it does for her every time she looks at it. It's set somewhere in the early fifties; there's a row of small terraced houses, and two women are leaning on a garden wall. They both have scarves around their heads and look as if they've just gotten back from an afternoon shift at work. But now they are taking time just to talk. A small scruffy boy with a huge smile is looking up at one of the women, but they ignore him; this is *their* time.

What Dianne finds so uplifting about the picture is that as she looks at it she imagines herself in that garden, eavesdropping on the conversation . . .

> *One woman is complaining because her husband seems to be dying of flu but the second he gets into bed suddenly recovers wonderfully and wants sex. The other throws her head back and laughs before she shares that her teenage son has stopped using language; he grunts his way around the house, and won't be seen dead with her outside of it. Just then in my mind's eye I see that the brand-new mom from the house along the terrace ventures into her garden and one of the older women shouts across three garden walls, "How's the little one, love?" The younger woman looks up red-eyed, and says, "He just won't sleep; he cries all night. I haven't slept since half-past two." The old hands laugh, "Listen, my love, make sure he's fed, warm, and dry—but don't pick him up every time he cries; if you do, you'll be doing it when he's thirty!" The young mom smiles, then laughs, and makes her way back to do battle with a four-week-old, but I sense her head is held a little higher.*

The conversation—the laughter—was liberating. We're not naive enough to believe those were the "golden days," but they did have one great advantage then: families normally lived closer than they do today. You tended to bring up your children surrounded by other mothers—your own mother, aunts, grandmothers, and friends. Knowledge and experience were passed on as well as something far more important: the understanding that whatever you were going through with your kids had been gone through before. You were neither unique in your success nor, more important, alone in your failure.

From what they tell us, most mothers don't want clever answers, and they certainly don't want clever answers from those who pretend they've got it all figured out. What they want most of all is for another mother to whisper to them, "This isn't just you. We've all been there, done that, and worn the T-shirt." One mom said:

> *I discovered I could handle almost all motherhood could throw at me so long as somebody could reassure me when I felt I'd screwed it up completely and ruined my kids' lives forever, that probably there had been other children who gave up violin after the first lesson, got caught smoking behind the bathrooms in school, and altered their report card on the way home.*

The good thing about this particular pressure is that we can do something about it. But to achieve this we have to realize that two of the most helpful words we can hear when we are doubting our ability as parents are, "me too." We somehow have to learn to share not just our successes but also our failures with others. The strange thing is that when we do, we find we don't depress those parents—we make their day!

Pressure Number Three: The Experts

Since we write books on family life and run seminars on parenting we acknowledge that we're part of the problem, but we have a proliferation of gurus on the family. These men and women often have a lot to teach us, and we would do well to consider what they say. Without doubt parenting is harder today than in previous generations, and we need all the help we can get. But the problem comes when we take what they say too seriously. By this we mean attaching to their advice the status of infallibility. The difficulty with this is there will always be somebody talking about some aspect of parenting and suggesting ideas that either it's too late for us to try, or we know in our heart just won't work in our situation. One mother put it like this, "Every time I hear a parenting expert giving a 'foolproof' way to deal with kids, I try it, only to discover that mine are the exception to the rule."

Take a common example. Most experts agree that it's unwise to pick up your newborn baby every time she cries and, even worse, to allow that to get to the stage where she sleeps in your bed when she's a toddler. There are many good reasons that's not a good idea, not least in the area of your ongoing sanity. But the truth is that there are millions of perfectly well-adjusted kids whose mothers did exactly that. These moms tried hanging around outside the bedroom door while their babies yelled their heads off, but they just couldn't do it. So what? Are those moms condemned to believe that they have ruined forever their child's chance of developing independence? Well, if you are one of them, hang on, because there's sure to be a guru out there who says, "The best way to build a sense of security in your child is to pick her up every time she cries."

We are not saying we don't need help as parents. We spend a fair part of our lives organizing parenting courses. It's just that when we've read the books, listened to the pediatrician, been to the seminars, and watched the parenting videos, we have to decide what works for *us*. And above all we need to remember that children are people, not machines. We sometimes wish it were different, but every mother has to be ready to put past failures behind her, try new things, and sometimes pray and hope for the best because every child is different and we are learning all the time. The other day Dianne was speaking at a seminar, and she related the following recollection.

When Dianne was six months pregnant with Katie she remembers saying, "I'm not sure I'm ready to have this baby." She is confident that many women have felt like that, but she says the really strange thing is that now she has more than twenty years of parenting behind her; she's gotten two kids through teething, toddlerhood, and the terrible teens; she has spoken to tens of thousands of people on parenting issues; and yet, if she was pregnant tomorrow, she can still imagine saying, "Rob, I don't think I'm ready to have this baby."

Perhaps that is not so strange for she is not at all sure that we can "learn" motherhood, we can only experience it, only feel it.

We're not saying that learning parenting skills or reading books on bringing up children are not helpful; we have benefited enormously by doing exactly that. It's just that sometimes we can be overwhelmed by the experts and all the advice. We believe that many moms spend their lives feeling as if they are utter failures. Some friends of ours went to visit relatives who lived hundreds of miles from us. The couple they were visiting was going through some minor hassles with their kids, and when our friends happened to say they knew us, these people commented, "Oh, the ones who write books on parenting? I suppose their kids are perfect." Dianne said, "We should invite them to come and stay for a couple of days: they won't stop laughing for a month."

Pressure Number Four: It Would Be a Great Job If It Wasn't for the Children.

So many of the mothers who write to us say they feel like failures and wish they could rewind the tape and have another run at parenthood. It seems to us that the great problem with bringing up children is that it's so unfair. The first child is normally quite a test, but you read a couple of books, talk to friends, and eventually you feel you're beginning to get the hang of it. And that's what lures you into having the second—you think you're an expert now. The problem is that heaven in its humor looks up the kind of child it sent you last time and now delivers one that is the opposite in every characteristic. The first one used to look scared when you raised your voice; this one laughs. Number one used to love coloring in books; number two loves coloring on friends' wallpaper. The first one slept like a baby; this one wants to go dancing before he's three.

And if we're not careful we think, *I must have lost it as a parent. What's happened to me?* The truth is that probably nothing has happened; we are just going through some of the traumas that, if they were honest, most parents, including the "experts" would admit to. Of course you may not think you are a failure; in fact, you may believe you are motherhood's own success story. Even now as you sit reading this book, coffee in hand, your new baby is gurgling happily as if to say, "Don't you worry about that next feeding, and this diaper is just fine." Your toddler has just inserted the final piece in a jigsaw that Toys 'R Us marked "for children ages 10–13," and your teenager is whistling as he finishes the dishes. Forgive us if we are about to shatter any dearly held illusions, and we are sure you are a wonderful mother, but our honest belief after observing thousands of families is that you just got lucky. Our advice is, don't be tempted to have a fourth.

A Tale of Two Children

There's a gap of three years between our two children. Katie was our first, and she was a typical compliant child. The first thing Katie did when she came into the world was to apologize to the midwife for being a little late. Katie was just glad to be on board. She lay on her back and gurgled as you changed her diaper, she loved to play store, math was a delight, she was kind to animals, and for the vast proportion of that period Dianne and I thought we were the perfect parents. We tutted to each other as we watched other toddlers having tantrums in the aisles of supermarkets. Sometimes, with hardly concealed glee, we pointed out to other parents where they might be going wrong with their offspring.

And then Lloyd came into our lives. Lloyd did not apologize to the midwife for being late. In fact Lloyd did not apologize for anything. He did not say sorry when he was three for removing the bottom can of beans from a display in the grocery store that took the Heinz rep a week to construct. He did not say sorry when he was five for urinating in a milk bottle in Mrs. Cleverly's kitchen, or for not telling us he had done it until we had finished our coffee. Well, actually, Lloyd did say "sorry" but it was one of those say-it-until-you-mean-it "sorrys."

The truth is that each of these children is unique, and they can change. Try not to break your heart over that child who is testing you daily and don't take the compliant one for granted either;

there may be a little rebellion to come there too. Somebody put it well: "Don't read your child's report cards as though they are a prophecy of their future lives." In other words, don't read the score at half-time.

You Ain't Seen Nothing Yet

Talking of rebellion gets us into a stage of a child's life that is just perfect for making a mother feel guilty—the teenage years. If you have toddlers, we don't for one moment minimize the task you have on your hands. It was Bill Cosby who said he could conquer the world if he could mobilize about two hundred aggressive two-year-olds. And we too have stood rooted to the spot and red-faced in the aisle of a supermarket as our toddler has created mayhem because he couldn't have that bag of candy. The only thing we would say is that if you think this is tough, you ain't seen nothing yet. And the reason for this is that no matter how difficult your toddler is, when they are small you still have a measure of control— you can bundle him up and get him home. But the day may come when a fifteen-year-old will look you in the eye and say, "No." That can be scary.

And the problem is that, as parents, we are used to protecting our children, to making life right for them. But as they get older we find we cannot do that in quite the same way; we simply do not have the same measure of control. They may choose friends we think will be a bad influence on them; they may leave homework undone, or start smoking; they may decide when they are eighteen they want to be a rock-and-roll singer whereas we always dreamed of their becoming a doctor. And we think, *How has this happened? Where did I go wrong?*

It is rare to meet a parent of teenagers who does not feel, in some way, a failure. No matter how much we read on the topic, no matter how many television programs we watch on parenting issues, we still believe what we are going through with our teenager is unique. A mother came up to us after one of our recent seminars. She looked troubled and obviously needed to talk. She explained that she was very concerned about her son. It seemed he'd undergone a character change. He had always been outgoing and affectionate, poured his heart out as soon as he got home from school every day. She had felt very close to him. And then he hit thirteen.

She said it was as if somebody "had flicked a switch." Her son seemed to change overnight. He became distant and withdrawn. Whereas before he would love to join in with whatever the family was doing, now he refused—and none too politely. He seemed to resent his parents. He shrank back when they touched him and said he hated his mother's cooking. He spent long hours in his room and grunted when she tried to get through to him. The only time he looked alive was when he was talking to his friends on the phone, but he soon got back to his sullen mode when he put the receiver down.

The woman sitting before me was genuinely grieving. She felt she must have done something terribly wrong when her son was young that had led to this change of character. Rob told her a story that he has related to thousands of mothers:

> *Some years ago I was interviewing a very eminent child psychologist and said to him, "Many parents of teenagers feel like failures. Do you have anything to say to people like this?" The good doctor didn't hesitate. He said, "I believe when a child reaches thirteen, hormonal changes occur in his or her body which cause them to blast into outer space. And then all communication with the satellite dies. They will only grunt at you. My advice to the parents of teenagers is just get them through those teenage years. Don't try to do much more than that. Fight as few battles as you possibly can. And then when they are about twenty, you'll begin getting signals from out there—they are still alive. And most of them land."*

And suddenly the mother in front of us started to smile; we sensed it was not with humor but with sheer relief. It had dawned on her that what she was going through was not *just her*. She didn't mind a battle; she just wanted to be sure that she wasn't the only mother in the war.

Of course sometimes it's more serious than that. Sometimes our children break our hearts. We think now of a mother we know sitting with her daughter in a jail cell. She is saying to her, "Rachel, I don't understand for a moment what you have done but I will always love you." That mom loved that girl so much it hurt.

The other night we were watching *Larry King Live* when Billy Graham came on. He told of the years of heartache he and his wife Ruth endured because of the behavior of one of their children. His son eventually came through that rocky time, and Ruth has written a book about it called *Prodigals and Those Who Love Them.*[5] But again it is the guilt that is crushing. We feel responsible even when our children are obviously old enough to make their own decisions. We ask, "Where did I go wrong?" The answer is often, "Nowhere." That's not to say that we have been perfect parents, or that we wouldn't like to have done some things differently. No, it's deeper than that. It's an acknowledgment that the day comes when we can't control them. Our children make choices.

Guilt is an occupational hazard of parenthood, but maybe we can gradually loosen its hold on us. So let the last word go to a mom of two who sent me this wonderful offering:

> *Mother-guilt is attached to the umbilical cord, but it stays with you for life.*
>
> *You feel guilty about what you do and guilty about what you don't do.*
>
> *Guilty when you leave them and guilty when you pick them up.*

*Guilty about what they eat, what they don't
eat, and even what they might eat.*

*The guilt gets you at night, on the train,
standing in the school playground, and especially
when you've left them when you have a break.*

*Then it usually gets attached to your purse
and leads you to a toy shop.*

*What mothers need is a jury of twelve good
and true mothers to stand up and say, "Not
guilty, your Honor."*

We like that piece because it tells us we can't be perfect parents. The most any of us can do is to give the task of parenthood our very best effort. Remember the *Sixty-Second Wisdom* from an older mother: "Don't take all the credit; don't take all the blame." There is a story of a man of eighty-two who was sentenced to seventeen years' imprisonment. As the judge read the punishment, the defendant said, "Your Honor, I'll be almost a hundred by the time I finish; I'll never make it." The judge hesitated, looked over the top of his half-rimmed spectacles, and said, "Do what you can."

It's not a bad principle for motherhood.

Sixty-Second Wisdom

60 Don't try to control them. If you fail, you'll never see them again; if you succeed, you'll never get rid of them.

60 Don't ever give up; sometimes prodigals come home.

60 Tell your kids every day, "I love you."

60 If you want to get a child who's almost asleep fully awake, try skipping two pages of a bedtime story.

Things Mothers Say . . .

- He lives away from home now, but if you know where he is, and he keeps in touch, your mind can be at rest. All he needs to do is give a quick call and say, "Hi Mom, I'm OK." Most times he says, "I've got no news," and I'll say, "That's fine, I'm just pleased you've phoned."

- As soon as Ben was passed to me in the delivery room, I knew he had Down's syndrome. Nobody needed to tell me. I loved him straightaway, and my fierce desire to protect him was there immediately. The thoughts came tumbling, *Would I be an object of sympathy?* I didn't want people to feel sorry for me because he wasn't what they call "normal"; that would be a rejection of my son.

- When Lynne got married and got her first apartment, she brought a real smile to my face. "Mom," she said on the phone one day, "we've had the gas bill, the electric bill, and the car tax all at once. You've no *idea* what it's like when they all come in together."

Like Mother, Like Daughter

I'm forty my next birthday, but Mom still asks:

- "Will you be long?"

- "Are you warm enough?"

- "Can't you eat something that's good for you?"

- "Where are your slippers?"

- "Isn't it your bedtime?"

And I say, "Yes, Mom," "No, Mom," or "I'm fine, Mom."

. . . So why does it unnerve me when I've heard myself say all these things to my teenage daughter in the last twelve hours and she's replied in exactly the same way?

Wendy

The Amnesia of Motherhood

- Helps us forget the pain of childbirth (almost) but remember their eyes seemingly fixed on our face a few moments afterward.

- Helps us forget the fights over junk food but remember cheeks and noses covered in chocolate ice cream.

- Helps us forget the clinging and crying at the preschool door or the frustration of trying to find the right school but sit down with the memories when we find that pile of crumpled, faded paintings ten years later.

- Helps us forget the arguments, the hurtful words, and slammed doors but remember bursting with pride when they left for college or their first job and how we tried not to cry when we cleaned their empty bedroom.

Then suddenly we need to remember all those things we forgot and try to imagine what it's like for her. A new mother in a new way in a new age. Remembering that the feeling, the secret knowledge, the unique experience of mothering will never be forgotten.

She would feel her throat swell at the memory of banana sandwiches, and in the winter the smell of warm buttered toast almost made her cry. Sometimes she wondered whether it was her own childhood she mourned or the childhood of her children.

Alice Thomas Ellis, *The Other Side of the Fire*

CHAPTER EIGHT

When a Mother Lets Go

One of the most inspired titles we have ever come across in a book on raising children is called *Parenting Isn't for Cowards*. But it seems to us there is something more difficult than parenting: it is *not* parenting. It is the process of letting go.

We dream of the day when our children are grown, and then suddenly they *are*. A mother wrote to best-selling author Erma Bombeck. She said:

> *"I know you've written about the empty-nest syndrome, that lonely period after the children are grown and gone. Right now I'm up to my eyeballs in laundry and muddy boots. The baby is teething; the boys are fighting. My husband just called and said to eat without him, and my diet has crashed. Tell me about it again, will you?"*

This was Erma Bombeck's reply:

> *Okay. One of these days you'll straighten up the boys' bedroom neat and tidy: bumper stickers discarded, bedspread tucked and smooth, hangers in the closet. Animals caged. And you'll say out loud, "Now I want it to stay that way." And it will. You'll say, "I want complete privacy on the phone.*

No dancing around. No demolition crews. Silence! Do you hear?" And you'll have it.

No more plastic tablecloths stained with spaghetti, no more gates to stumble over at the bottom of the stairs, no more anxious nights under a vaporizer tent. No more rubber bands for pony tails or wet knotted shoestrings.

Imagine. A lipstick with a point on it. No baby-sitter for New Year's Eve. Washing only once a week. Having your teeth cleaned without a baby on your lap. No parent-teacher meetings. No blaring radios. No one washing her hair at 11:00 o'clock at night.

Think about it. No more sloppy oatmeal kisses. No more tooth fairy. No giggles in the dark. No knees to heal. No responsibility.

One of these days, you'll shout, "Why don't you kids grow up and act your age?" And they will.[6]

If it's any comfort, a tear has just bounced off the word processor! But we'd better not get too emotional about it all, simply remember that this is the end goal—to let them go. This is what it's all about.

But it is hard. The great difficulty for every mother is that you've spent all your life protecting your children from danger, guarding them, making sure that no one could ever do them harm—physical or emotional. But letting them go exposes them to all of this. When our daughter Katie was eleven and went into the city shops on her own for the first time, we both followed her. Rob nearly got arrested diving in and out of shop doorways. But we can't always protect them from pain, or failure, or from some boy or girl breaking their heart. The truth is that these things are a necessary part of the very process of moving into adulthood.

We may try to control our children, but ultimately we cannot do it. John White, psychiatrist and author of *Parents in Pain,* put it like this, "You cannot control another human being, even if that human being is your own child. You do not have the right to. You may discipline and teach; you may train; you may point out the right course; you may 'shape behavior patterns'; you may reason; you may plead. But you cannot and may not ever control."[7]

One day a woman walked in a garden. The day was wonderful, and the flowers were prolific. She could smell the promise of summer in the wind. And then she saw it. At first she thought it was a dead leaf hanging on from the winter, but then she moved closer and saw it was a chrysalis. And suddenly it moved. The baby butterfly inside was trying to get out. She found it almost distressing watching its pathetic efforts and finally she could stand it no more. She rushed indoors, got a small knife, and gently pried apart the hard skin of the chrysalis so the butterfly could escape. She saw a wing emerge and then another. It was a beautiful sight; this young one emerging to adulthood. And then it tried to fly but fell to the floor. It tried again and again. This was strange. A butterfly that couldn't even get off the ground.

Later the woman related to a friend what had happened. The friend, who knew about these things, explained: "I'm sure you meant well, but when you stepped in to help, you stopped a process that nature had designed to strengthen that insect's wings. The butterfly was meant to struggle inside the chrysalis; it was supposed to find it hard going for a while, because in the very act of fighting to get out, the wings become strong."

We remember so many times running to sort things out for our children. Rob has finished off geography projects and love letters and in later years kept irate bank managers at bay. But Dianne has said time and time again, "Rob, you must let them go. They have to learn themselves—even if it hurts a little." It is the principle of the butterfly.

Almost ten years ago we received a letter from a woman. Her husband had left her for somebody else, and she had borne alone the responsibility of bringing up their children. It must be even harder for a single-parent mom to let go, but in the letter was a poem that convinced me that this mom understood what so many mothers have told us—that if you let them go you generally keep them.

> *She is gone.*
> *The child I once knew*
> *And in her place a woman.*
> *Vulnerable*

Lacking polish
Needing assurance perhaps
But nevertheless
A woman.

The pain of her birth into womanhood
Was every bit as great as the pain of her birth
The more so perhaps because of its
Suddenness.

Then there were months of waiting,
Of preparation,
Now in a day
Separation.
She's gone.

She's gone
And I must let her go.

Time now for painful rebuilding
Where innocence—now knowledge
Where wondering—now certainty
Where hesitancy—now assurance
Where once childlike trust
Now I must accept a woman's vulnerability.

Viewpoints considered—decisions made—
without me.
Ideas formulated carefully
Girlhood pushed back—

womanhood embraced
As she steps from my arms into his.

But I will wait
Not in desperation—but patiently.
For she may need me yet
As man needs man
And woman needs another woman.
And we will walk together she and I
Side by side.
For my child is gone
and in her place—
A woman.

Dianne (very graciously, she says!) allows Rob the last word . . .

As I finish writing this book today, I will go to visit my mother. And when I do I will find that time has performed its great trick and the child has become the parent and the mother the child. Sometimes I arrive at supper time and if so, I take over the task of feeding her. I will put food on a spoon and hold it to her mouth, encouraging her to finish the plate. Then I will ask her, "Would you like a drink?"

And when I have done that, I will talk to her. Oh, not talk that you would understand—she is long past that now—but rather the kind of conversation she had with me as she put me to bed when I was small. And then I will tuck the bedclothes in around her, and straighten the top sheet, bend to kiss her and say, "Shall we say prayers?" And then a strange thing will happen: this woman who can scarcely string three words together will take my hand and in a strong voice say word-for-word the prayer she said with me each night as she put me to bed, "Our Father, who art in heaven, hallowed be thy name . . ." And if I close my eyes, I can imagine her there—all those years ago—young and pretty, and hassled, and praying for her children.

She was not a perfect mother. But she loved and did her best. Those two qualities elevate ordinary mothers to superhuman status, which is why children scrawl the same words on Mother's Day cards the world over. I am no exception to this rule and before I leave her, I always go through the same routine: "You're the best mother in the world; did you know that?" And a smile comes to her lips, and she says, "Who says so?" and I reply, "Oh, *everybody* knows it."

Notes

1. James Finn Garner, *Politically Correct Bedtime Stories* (London: Souvenir Press, Ltd., 1994).
2. Kate Saunders, cited in Matthew and Victoria Glendinning, eds., *Sons and Mothers* (London: Virago Press, 1997).
3. Rob Parsons, *The Sixty-Minute Father* (Nashville: Broadman & Holman, 1996), 21–31.
4. Mary Bourgoin, "Working Mothers—Supermoms or Drones," *The Washington Post.*
5. Ruth Bell Graham, *Prodigals and Those Who Love Them* (Grand Rapids, Mich.: Baker Book House, 1999).
6. Erma Bombeck, *Family—The Ties that Bind . . . and Gag!* (Fawcett Books, 1998).
7. John White, *Parents in Pain: A Book of Comfort and Grief* (Downer Grove, Ill.: InterVarsity Press, 1979).